Hamilton Troll
CURRICULUM

AWARD-WINNING EDUCATIONAL SERIES

Contents

Reading Comprehension

Language Arts

Math Worksheets

Science Projects

Fun Stuff

Answer Sheets

www.HamiltonTrollBooks.com

Hamilton Troll's Curriculum Worksheets & Activity Book

Manufactured in the United States of America.

ISBN-13: 978-1-941345-25-2 Paperback

Educational curriculum, games and designs by Kathleen J. Shields
Character Illustrations by Leigh A. Klug
Background cover illustrations by Carol W. Bryant

ERIN GO BRAGH
Publishing

www.ErinGoBraghPublishing.com

To receive updates or purchase additional books, please visit:

www.HamiltonTroll.com

READING

COMPREHENSION

QUIZZES

Hamilton Troll meets
Pink Light Sprite

Quiz

1) Where does Hamilton Troll live?
 a) tree
 b) shoe
 c) hole
 d) box

2) What is Hamilton Troll afraid of?
 a) loud thunder
 b) rain flooding his home
 c) bright lightning
 d) strong wind

3) Where does Hamilton Troll go for safety?
 a) Hide Away Flop
 b) big leaf plants
 c) elephant ear leaves
 d) all of the above

4) Why can Hamilton Troll see Pink Light Sprite
 a) her wings got wet and she couldn't fly
 b) she was resting from a long trip
 c) she wanted to make a new friend
 d) she wanted to be alone

5) What does Pink Light Sprite suggest Hamilton Troll do?
 a) move to a new location
 b) don't worry about the rain
 c) transplant the leaves near his home
 d) use a mushroom as a door

Name: _____   Date: _____

Hamilton Troll meets Skeeter Skunk

1) What does Skeeter Skunk want to do?
   a) Eat flowers
   b) Spray everyone he can
   c) Watch the big game
   d) Play in the stick nut game

2) What did the friends NOT try to solve Skeeter Skunk's problem?
   a) Cover his eyes
   b) Cover his smell
   c) Cover his ears
   d) Cover his mouth

3) Why did they cover Skeeter Skunk with flowers?
   a) They were trying to make him look pretty
   b) They wanted to play dress-up
   c) They were trying to cover the smell of his spray
   d) They wanted to hide him in the flowers

4) What did the shy bunny say?
   a) When I eat these red berries I become a real stinker.
   b) I get shy around others and my cheeks turn red.
   c) I was so embarrassed I ran off to hide.
   d) Whenever I play stick-nut I get afraid.

5) In the end, what was it that kept Skeeter from spraying everyone?
   a) He was out of spray
   b) He was tired
   c) He had made friends
   d) He didn't want to spray them

Hamilton Troll meets

Barney Bee

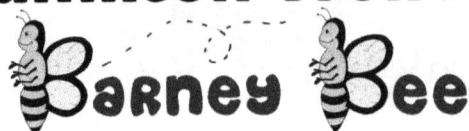

1) What was Barney Bee doing when Hamilton Troll found him?
 a) Flying around
 b) Buzzing a neat song
 c) Eating pollen from a flower
 d) Playing with other bees

2) Why did Barney Bee fly past the red flowers?
 a) Because he wanted to get to the other side
 b) Because they didn't smell good
 c) Because bees are color blind and he didn't see them
 d) Because the pink ones taste much better

3) What does Barney Bee say to explain why he doesn't have friends?
 a) All the bees are to busy
 b) All the birds are to fast
 c) All the critters are afraid to get stung
 d) All of the above

4) Why did Barney Bee fall out of the sky?
 a) His wings were tired
 b) His wings couldn't hold his weight
 c) The wind pushed him down
 d) There was a nice flower on the ground

5) What does Barney need to do to keep flying?
 a) Eat less pollen
 b) Exercise
 c) Play
 d) All of the above

Name: _____ Date: _____

Hamilton Troll meets Chatterton Squirrel

1) What were Chatterton Squirrel's parents teaching him?
 a) How to fly
 b) How to run across tree limbs
 c) How to leap from one tree to the next
 d) How to talk like a squirrel

2) Who went first to show how it was done?
 a) Mother
 b) Father
 c) Brother
 d) Sister

3) Why wouldn't Chatterton do this task?
 a) He was afraid of falling
 b) He didn't feel like it
 c) He didn't need to
 d) He already knew how to

4) What did Hamilton sit on to watch the squirrels practice?
 a) A red rock
 b) A small log
 c) A green clover
 d) A crimson clover

5) What did Hamilton Troll do to help Chatterton learn?
 a) Draw a line in the dirt
 b) Make big purple X's on the ground
 c) Suggest Chatterton practice on the ground first
 d) All of the above

Hamilton Troll meets
ELWOOD WOODPECKER

Quiz

1) What gave Elwood Woodpecker the headache?
 a) Pecking on petrified wood
 b) Playing too many video games
 c) He got hit on the head
 d) None of the above

2) Who did Hamilton and Elwood visit to learn about petrified wood?
 a) Rachel Raccoon
 b) Pink Light Sprite
 c) Beaver Brothers
 d) Skeeter Skunk

3) How did the petrified wood get there?
 a) Floated down the river
 b) Dropped off a tree
 c) Rolled down a hill
 d) All of the above

4) What happened to Boswell Beaver when he first learned about petrified wood?
 a) He tripped over it and hurt his foot
 b) He made it into a beaver dam
 c) He ran off to find out more about it
 d) He chipped his front tooth on it

5) What does Hamilton Troll do now that he knows what petrified wood is?
 a) He keeps it to himself
 b) He hangs out with the beaver brothers and goes swimming
 c) He tells the others about what he learned
 d) He spends the rest of the day with Elwood Woodpecker

Hamilton Troll meets
DINOSAURS

Quiz

1) What did Hamilton Troll find that led him on this journey?
 a) A rock shaped like a dinosaur
 b) A fossil that looked like a seashell
 c) A rock that looked like a flower
 d) A fossil shaped like a mouse

2) Where did the beaver brothers
   take Hamilton Troll?
 a) A school
 b) A museum
 c) A computer
 d) A library

3) How did Hamilton Troll find
   himself in dinosaur time?
 a) A time machine
 b) A magic door
 c) A river ride
 d) A dream

4) How big were the footprints?
 a) Twice as big as Hamilton
 b) As tall as a tree
 c) Ten times longer than him
 d) Five times his length, six, maybe eight

5) What did the mama dinosaur teach Hamilton Troll?
 a) Dinosaurs are all friendly
 b) All dinosaurs eat plants
 c) There are plant eaters and meat eaters
 d) She rules the land

Hamilton Troll meets Whitaker Owl

Quiz

1) What are Whitaker Owl's parents teaching him?
 a) How to fly
 b) How to hoot
 c) How to catch food
 d) None of the above

2) What does Hamilton Troll think Whitaker sounds like?
 a) A bear
 b) An Owl
 c) A cat
 d) A ghost

3) What happens that upsets everyone?
 a) A bear comes near
 b) A ghost appears
 c) His parents fly away
 d) A bat flies by

4) What did the bear say?
 a) Do you taste like chicken?
 b) You sound like a ghost.
 c) These woods are haunted.
 d) Can we play together?

5) What does Whitaker do to save the night?
 a) He flies by the bear hooting like a ghost
 b) He asks a couple ghosts to scare the bear away
 c) He asks his parents for help
 d) He screams out loud

Hamilton
Troll meets
Rudy Rat

Quiz

1) Why is Rosa Raccoon crying?
  a) she lost the Stick-Nut game
  b) Rudy Rat fell and hurt himself
  c) she was lost and couldn't get home
  d) Rudy Rat was being mean

2) What did Rudy Rat do?
  a) he took Susie's flower
  b) he ate Billy's lunch
  c) he tripped little Tim in the hall
  d) all of the above

3) What does Hamilton want to do about Rudy Rat?
  a) punish him
  b) talk to him
  c) be mean to him
  d) none of the above

4) What do the kids do to Rudy Rat?
  a) bully him back
  b) make him run away
  c) invite him to play
  d) scare him and laugh

5) What does PAWS stand for?
  a) Prepare, Answer, Write, Spell
  b) Pretend, Approach, Welcome, Smile
  c) Pause, Approach, Welcome, Smile
  d) Pause, Answer, Welcome, Sing

Hamilton Troll

and the Case of the

Missing Home

1) What scares Hamilton out of his home?
 a) a bear growling
 b) a loud sound
 c) a screaming cat
 d) a clap of thunder

2) What happened to his tree?
 a) it fell down
 b) it was cut down
 c) it disappeared like magic
 d) none of the above

3) What does Rachel Raccoon find out?
 a) the tree is gone forever
 b) it was taken to a human's home
 c) it is going to be used for Christmas
 d) all of the above

4) What does Hamilton Troll want to do?
 a) go find a new home
 b) run off and cry
 c) tell everyone about it
 d) go visit his tree

5) What was the tree used for?
 a) making furniture
 b) building a beaver dam
 c) decoration for Christmas
 d) firewood

Name: _____   Date: _____

Hamilton Troll meets FIONA THE DOG

Quiz

1) What items are going missing?
 a) Rudy Rat's hat
 b) Merle Mouse's mat
 c) Amara's broom
 d) all of the above

2) How did Rudy Rat feel about his missing hat?
 a) very sad
 b) confused
 c) angry
 d) lonely

3) What happens to Hamilton Troll?
 a) his ladder goes missing
 b) he gets carried away
 c) he meets Fiona the dog
 d) all of the above

4) What does Hamilton Troll discover?
 a) all of the items were taken by the wind
 b) everyone's things were broken
 c) Fiona took everyone's things
 d) everyone misplaced their stuff

5) What does Hamilton do to solve this?
 a) He tells Fiona she is bad
 b) He tells everyone what Fiona did
 c) He takes his ladder home
 d) He suggests Fiona return the stuff

Name: _____   Date: _____

Hamilton Troll meets
Starlit Troll

Quiz

1) How did Starlit Troll arrive?
 a) She floated down the river
 b) She rode on a dog
 c) She rode on a duck
 d) She floated on the wind

2) What is special troll sight?
 a) being able to see magic
 b) being able to see other trolls
 c) being able to see fairies
 d) all of the above

3) What does Hamilton plan for the day?
 a) a hike
 b) a picnic
 c) a concert
 d) a party

4) Why couldn't he find Starlit?
 a) She had been everywhere he went
 b) She was looking for him
 c) He wasn't where she was looking
 d) All of the above

5) What did Hamilton do when he found everyone had eaten his food?
 a) He filled with defeat
 b) He huffed at everyone
 c) He realized everyone thought they were invited.
 d) All of the above

Hamilton Troll
and the BIG RACE

1) What made Starlit Troll upset?
   a) He made fun of her.
   b) He hurt her.
   c) She misunderstood him.
   d) All of the above.

2) Who taught Hamilton troll about tree jumping?
   a) Starlit Troll
   b) Skeeter Skunk
   c) Chatterton Squirrel
   d) Whitaker Owl

3) How did Starlit troll get down the Rapids?
   a) She swam down them.
   b) She surfed them down.
   c) She tiptoed across.
   d) She ran over them.

4) Why did Hamilton lose the race?
   a) He was too slow.
   b) He cheated.
   c) He tripped and fell on a rock.
   d) He slowed down.

5) How did Hamilton troll solve his problem?
   a) He pouted
   b) He congratulated Starlit.
   c) He went to the party.
   d) He went to his hidden away flop.

LANGUAGE ARTS WORKSHEETS

WORD SCRAMBLE

The letters on the left will fill in the spots on the right. Use the word bank at the bottom for help.

KNIP TILGH TEPRIS

YEBRAN EBE

AAARM LODIMRALA

RKWTIAHE LOW

ELRME SOUME

DELOOW

REKETSE KKSUN

NILTAHOM LORTL

RTTTEOACNH

WORD BANK

AMARA ARMADILLO   BARNEY BEE
CHATTERTON   ELWOOD
HAMILTON TROLL   MERLE MOUSE
SKEETER SKUNK   WHITAKER OWL
PINK LIGHT SPRITE

Name: _____ Date: _____

Hamilton Troll meets

Barney Bee

Nouns

A noun is a word that names a person, place or thing. Cross off all the words on Barney Bee that are not nouns. Then write the nouns in the spaces below.

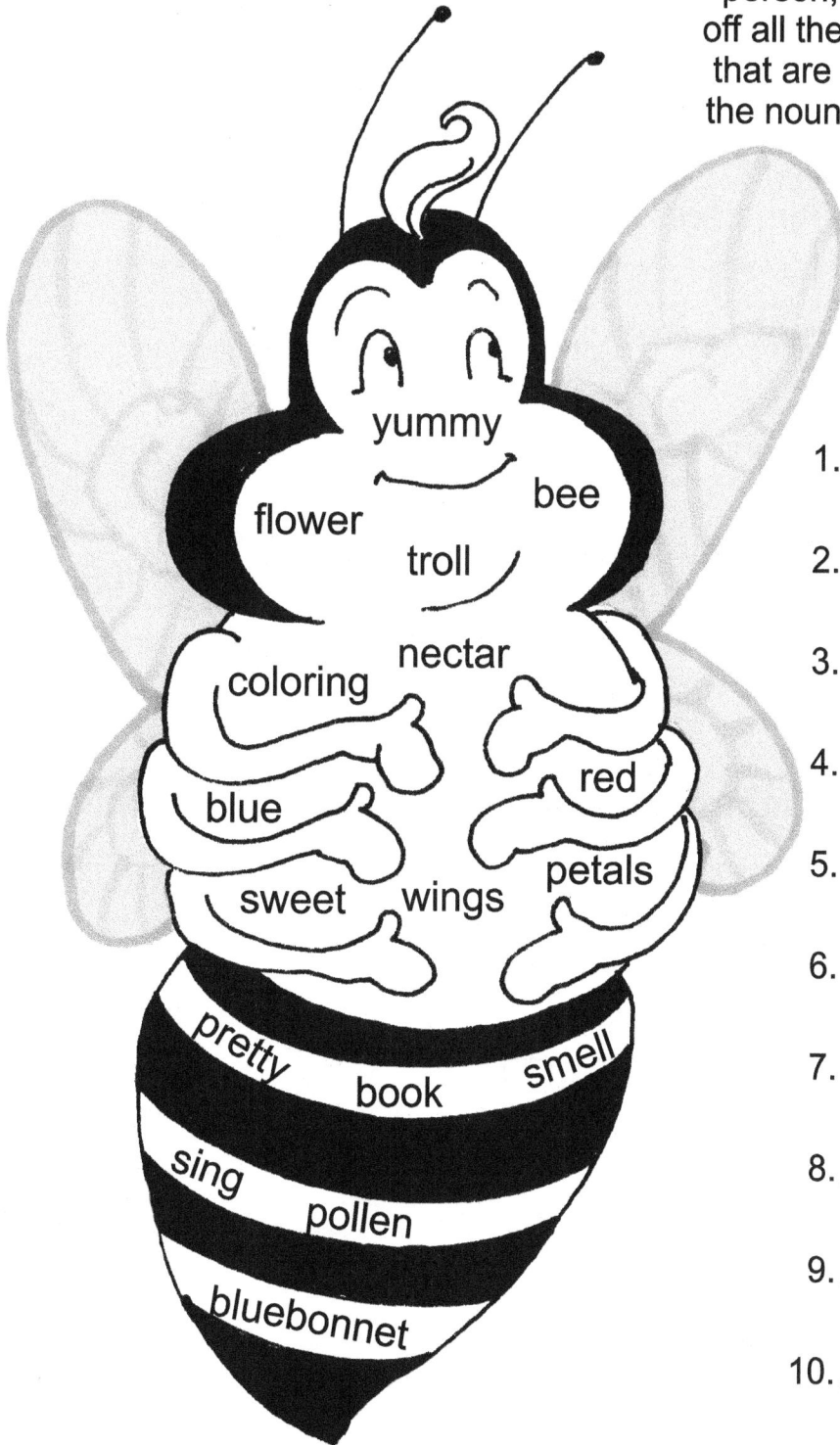

yummy

bee

flower

troll

nectar

coloring

blue

red

sweet   wings   petals

pretty

book   smell

sing

pollen

bluebonnet

1. _____

2. _____

3. _____

4. _____

5. _____

6. _____

7. _____

8. _____

9. _____

10. _____

Hamilton Troll meets
Barney Bee

Verbs

**A verb is a word
that shows action.**

Circle the verb that correctly completes each sentence.

1. Hamilton Troll dreams about having wings.

2. Hamilton tells Barney to exercise.

3. Barney runs and jumps each day.

4. Barney Bee falls out of the sky.

5. Barney skips over the red flowers.

Fill in the blank with the verb that best works in the sentence.

1. Barney Bee _____ to each flower.
    flies, runs

2. Hamilton Troll _____ with Barney.
    talks, plays

3. Barney _____ nectar.
    breathes, eats

4. Hamilton _____ with his friends.
    plays, sings

5. Barney _____ on a flower.
    rests, jumps

Name: _____ Date: _____

Hamilton Troll meets
Pink Light Sprite

Circle the adjective in each sentence.
Underline the noun it describes.

Adjectives

1. Hamilton Troll has red hair.

2. Hamilton Troll has brown eyes.

3. Pink Light Sprite has blonde hair.

4. Pink Light Spite had wet wings.

5. Hamilton moved big plants.

Tips to Remember:

An **adjective** is a word that describes a noun.

An **adjective** can come before the noun it describes.

A **noun** is a person, place or thing.

6. Hamilton's home filled with blue rain water.

7. Hamilton hid under big green leaves.

Name: _____   Date: _____

Hamilton Troll meets Skeeter Skunk

Noun, Verb or Adjective

In the blanks write whether the underlined word is a noun, verb or adjective.

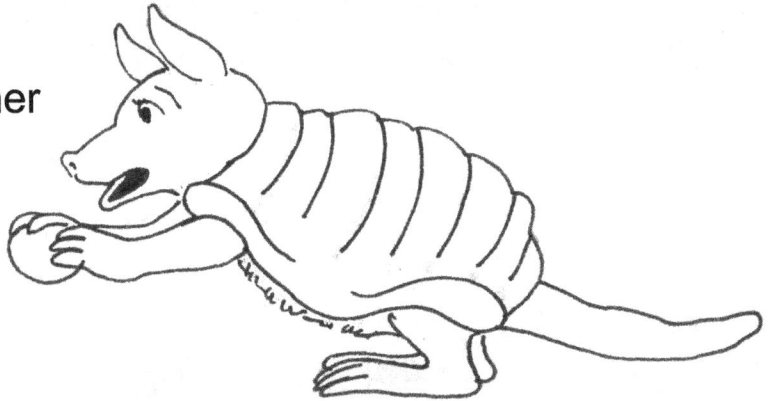

1. Amara Armadillo is a <u>catcher</u>. _____

2. The nut, in Stick-Nut, is a <u>hazelnut</u>. _____

3. The crowd <u>cheered</u> for Skeeter. _____

4. Skeeter Skunk was <u>afraid</u> of the nut. _____

5. Hamilton Troll <u>helped</u> Skeeter. _____

6. Amara Armadillo is <u>grey</u>. _____

7. Skeeter Skunk's spray is <u>stinky</u>. _____

8. A hazel nut is <u>yummy</u> to eat. _____

9. Skeeter <u>ran</u> as fast as a could. _____

10. Skeeter Skunk ate <u>flowers</u>. _____

Name _____ Date _____

In the blanks, write whether the underlined word is a noun, verb or adjective.

Noun, Verb or Adjective

1. <u>Hamilton Troll</u> lives in a hole. _____

2. Diggory Armadillo has a <u>hard</u> shell. _____

3. Skeeter Skunk <u>eats</u> flowers. _____

4. Chatterton is a <u>squirrel</u>. _____

5. Chatterton Squirrel <u>jumps</u> in the trees. _____

6. Skeeter is a <u>stinky</u> skunk. _____

7. Hamilton is a <u>friendly</u> troll. _____

8. Five animals above have a <u>tail</u>. _____

9. Everyone <u>sits</u> down. _____

10. Hamilton is a <u>green</u> troll. _____

Name _____ Date _____

Hamilton Troll
meet
FIONA THE DOG

Adjectives & Nouns

Circle the adjectives and cross out the nouns.

sad   happy

nice   pile

paws

friendly   nose

white dog

fast

curious   soft

eyes   fur

toys   pink

pointy ears

red tongue

Hamilton Troll meets
Barney Bee

Homophone

Homophones are words that sound alike but have different spellings and meanings.

An example would be; two, to, too and there, they're, their.

You can have **two** apples.

You can go **to** school.

You can do your homework **too**.

You can go **there**.

It is **their** idea.

They're going to go sing.

Fill in the blanks with the correct homophone to the right.

1. Out of _____ flowers, Barney _____ two.	**ate, eight**
2. Barney said, "_____ have pollen in my _____.	**I, eyes**
3. "Do you _____ why I can't fly?" Hamilton says, "_____."	**no, know**
4. The wind _____ Barney by a _____ colored flower.	**blue, blew**
5. There were many _____ or flowers but only one red _____.	**rose, rows**
6. "I can't _____ to see if Barney lost _____."	**wait, weight**
7. There were a _____ of blue flowers as far as he could _____.	**see, sea**
8. Barney _____ to a flower then sneezed like he had the _____.	**flu, flew**
9. Hamilton said, "I _____ you were _____ to the area."	**new, knew**
10. With _____ more player, the group _____ the Stick-Nut game.	**won, one**

Name: _____   Date: _____

Hamilton Troll meets Skeeter Skunk

Finish the Sentence

Read each sentence. Write the correct word on the line.

1. Skeeter Skunk wanted to _____ the game.

    say   way   play

2. They tried to hide the smell with _____.

    showers   flowers   powers

3. Skeeter Skunk is black and _____.

    white   right   light

4. They covered his _____ and said boo.

    ears   fears   cheers

5. Hamilton and Skeeter _____ the game.

    one   won   fun

Name _____ Date _____

Hamilton Troll meet *FIONA THE DOG*

Fill in the blanks with the word that best fits the sentence.

1. In the story, Fiona _____ Rudy Rat's hat.
   takes, breaks

2. Fiona the _____ has white fur.
   cat, dog

3. Fiona's favorite word is: _____
   Mine! , Yours.

4. Hamilton _____ on a toy fire truck.
   jumps, stands

5. Fiona _____ her family.
   hears, ignores

6. Fiona _____ Hamilton Troll.
   bites, licks

7. Hamilton and Fiona _____ the items.
   keep, return

8. Fiona put everything she took into a _____.
   hole, pile

9. Hamilton _____ on Fiona's back.
   rides, dances

10. Fiona wears a _____ bandana around her neck.
    blue, pink

Hamilton Troll is playing detective.

Help Hamilton Troll find the word that don't belong. Draw an **X** on the words in each group that do not match the word at the top.

Hamilton Troll lives in a hole.

live

jive live
hive love

Hamilton walks along the path.

walk

wakl wolk
walk welk

After it stopped raining, he came out.

after

ofter after
alter often

There were two rainbows.

were

week vere
were weer

Rhymes

A rhyme is a word that sounds similar to another. Like *blue / true*. Some words are long and so the rhyme is focused on the end of the word. Like *remember / December*

Pick the best rhyming word for the sentence.

1. Hamilton's a troll. He lives in a _____.
   hole, bowl

2. Rosa the racoon, slept under the _____.
   spoon, moon

3. The color is red, on top of his _____.
   bed, head

4. When Hamilton is sad, no body is _____.
   mad, glad

5. How would you know, when the wind will _____.
   blow, grow

6. When the tree is gone, it is bright at _____.
   yawn, dawn

7. The birds would fly, in the _____.
   try, sky

8. Rudy lost his hat, Merle lost his _____.
   mat, fat

9. They looked at the ground. They looked all _____.
   found, around

10. Fiona is sweet. She's quick on her _____.
    beat, feet

Name _____ Date _____

Hamilton Troll

meets

RUDY RAT

Right or Wrong

Read the sentences below and determine which is right and which is wrong? Write your answer in the blank. A sample has been done for you.

Rudy Rat is being mean to others. _____**wrong**_____

Rosa Racoon tells Hamilton Troll. _____**right**_____

1. Rudy Rat popped Rosa's mushroom ball. _____

2. Rosa and the children invite Rudy to play. _____

3. Rudy Rat teases Diggory Armadillo. _____

4. Rudy trips little Timmy in the hall. _____

5. Hamilton asks the children to talk to Rudy. _____

Hamilton Troll
meets
Rudy Rat

Right or Wrong

Read the sentences below and determine which is right and which is wrong? Write your answer in the blank. A sample has been done for you.

1. A group of children push another child. _____

2. You ask a child who is alone to join you. _____

3. A child breaks another child's toys. _____

4. You ignore a child who is crying. _____

5. You put your PAWS together for friendship. _____

6. You let someone borrow a crayon. _____

7. You draw on someone else's drawing without

   asking for permission. _____

Hamilton Troll
meets

RUDY RAT

Right or Wrong

Read the sentences below and determine which is right and which is wrong? Write your answer in the blank. A sample has been done for you.

1. You introduce yourself to a new child. _____

2. You see a bully and tell a teacher. _____

3. Someone tells you to do something that you think may

   be wrong and you do it anyway. _____

4. You tell a child they would be cool if they picked on

   another child. _____

5. You tell your parents someone is being mean when they

   are not being mean. _____

Name _____ Date _____

Bees may be busy, but they still stop to smell the flowers.

What do you do to keep busy?

Write a list of 5 things you like to do in the spaces provided then explain it in full sentences below. *See example.*

Example:
1. <u>write</u>
1. <u>I like to write short stories.</u>

I like to:

1. _____
2. _____
3. _____
4. _____
5. _____

_____

_____

_____

_____

_____

_____

_____

Learn Cursive Writing

a b c d e f g h i j k l

m n o p q r s t u v w

x y z

A B C D E F G H I J

K L M N O P Q R

S T U V W X Y Z

Starting from the left and going to the right, trace the letters of the alphabet. Start with the first line on the left. Use the arrows to direct your pencil.

Then on the next page, practice your cursive writing. Note: the dotted line in the center is the half way point for your letters. Lowercase letters stay below the dotted line.

Hamilton Troll thinks this is a very important thing to learn.

Hello

Name: _____ Date: _____

Fill in the beginning consonant letter for each word.
Draw a line from the word to the matching picture.

_____ roll ●   ●

_____accoon ●   ●

_____ ouse ●   ●

_____ ee ●   ●

_____ quirrel ●   ●

_____ inosaur ●   ●

B D M R S T

CROSSWORD PUZZLE

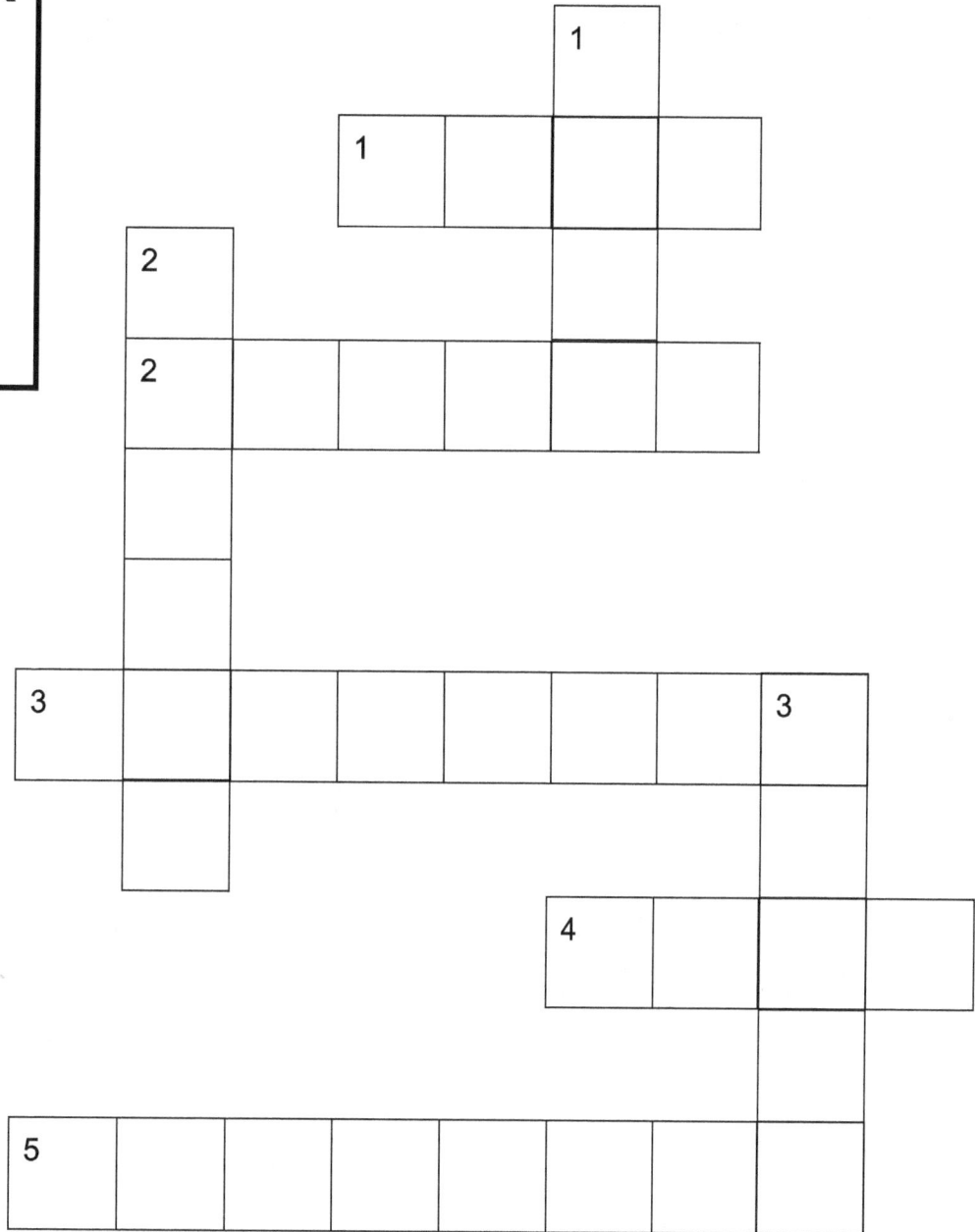

ACROSS

1. THE SIGN IS CALLED HIDE AWAY _____

2. BARNEY BEE LOVES _____

3. THE GAME THEY PLAY IS _____

4. WHITAKER OWL LEARNS TO _____

5. CHATTERTON IS A _____

DOWN

1. THE LEAVES MAKE

   THE SHAPE OF A _____

2. PINK LIGHT _____

3. HAMILTON IS A _____

HIDDEN MESSAGE

Color only the letters with a ♥ to read a secret message from Hamilton Troll

WYSIORPHUR

EMADKBRSEI

OGRPNEQASL

PJGRDEAZTFY

FTRIPEDNSDZ

Write the message here:

MATH

WORKSHEETS

Name: _____   Date: _____

Hamilton Troll meets

Barney Bee

Barney Bee now needs to keep track of how many flowers he eats per day if he wants to keep flying. Look at the chart to see how many flowers he ate from each day and what color they were. Then answer the questions below.

Day	Blue	Pink	Yellow
Day 1	4	4	3
Day 2	2	5	4
Day 3	0	6	5
Day 4	5	2	8

1. How many flowers did he eat from on day 2?

4. Did he eat any blue flowers on day 3?

2. How many blue flowers did he eat total?

5. On day 4 Barney Bee fell from the sky. What did he do different from the first three days?

3. How many pink and blue flowers did he eat on day 3?

Name: _____ Date: _____

Hamilton Troll meets

Math

1. How many stripes are on
   Barney Bee's tail?

2. How many stripes are white?

3. How many arms does
   Barney Bee have?

4. If there are 5 flowers and Barney eats
   nectar out of two, how many flowers does he have left?

5. To keep Barney flying, he needs to do 5 jumping jacks for every
   flower he eats from. How many flowers can he eat from if he
   does 25 jumping jacks?

Hamilton Troll meets Skeeter Skunk

Counting Frogs

Hamilton Troll and friends counted the cheering frogs at the Stick-Nut game for the last four days. Look at the chart to see how many frogs they saw each day. Then answer the questions.

Cheering Frogs	
Day	Frogs
Day 1	5
Day 2	8
Day 3	10
Day 4	7

How many frogs did Hamilton and friends see in all?

_____ frogs in all

How many fewer frogs did they see on day 1 versus day 4?

_____ fewer frogs

How many more frogs did Hamilton and friends see in day 3 versus day 1?

_____ more frogs

Name _____ Date _____

Math
Addition

1) How many fingers are visible on Hamilton's waving hand? _____

2) How many fingers are on one of your hands? _____

3) Add your answers, how many fingers
   are on Hamilton's hand and your hand. _____

4) How many ears are on the bunnies above? _____

5) How many tails are on the animals above? _____

4) Add your answers, how many bunny
   ears and animal tails are there? _____

Name _____ Date _____

Math
Addition

1) How many squirrels are there above? _____

2) How many birds are there total? _____

3) Add the total of squirrels
   and birds together. _____

4) How many bugs are there? _____

5) Add how many bugs and
   squirrels there are total? _____

Name: _____ Date: _____

Hamilton Troll meets
ELWOOD WOODPECKER

1. How many stars does Elwood Woodpecker see?

2. How many flower petals are there total?

3. Looking at the pictures below, How many worms does Elwood Woodpecker get to eat?

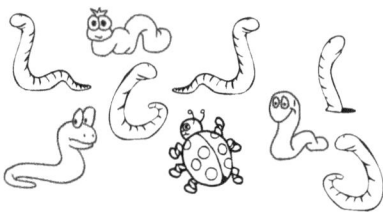

4. How many fish are swimming around the beaver brothers?

Hamilton Troll meets
ELWOOD WOODPECKER

1. If Elwood Woodpecker eats three worms. How many are left?

2. If Hamilton Troll picks 9 flowers and gives 3 to Elwood and 2 to Baxter Beaver, how many will he have left?

3. If Baxter and Boswell each cut down two trees, how many will be left standing in the scene below?

Name _____ Date _____

If you have
4 *apples*
and I have
4 *apples,*
the equation
would look like:

4 x 2 =

Merle Mouse is teaching
Hamilton Troll how to multiply.
Why don't you learn with him?

1 x 1 = 1	2 x 1 = 2	3 x 1 = 3	4 x 1 = 4	5 x 1 = 5
1 x 2 = 2	2 x 2 = 4	3 x 2 = 6	4 x 2 = 8	5 x 2 = 10
1 x 3 = 3	2 x 3 = 6	3 x 3 = 9	4 x 3 = 12	5 x 3 = 15
1 x 4 = 4	2 x 4 = 8	3 x 4 = 12	4 x 4 = 16	5 x 4 = 20
1 x 5 = 5	2 x 5 = 10	3 x 5 = 15	4 x 5 = 20	5 x 5 = 25
1 x 6 = 6	2 x 6 = 12	3 x 6 = 18	4 x 6 = 24	5 x 6 = 30
1 x 7 = 7	2 x 7 = 14	3 x 7 = 21	4 x 7 = 28	5 x 7 = 35
1 x 8 = 8	2 x 8 = 16	3 x 8 = 24	4 x 8 = 32	5 x 8 = 40
1 x 9 = 9	2 x 9 = 18	3 x 9 = 27	4 x 9 = 36	5 x 9 = 45
1 x 10 = 10	2 x 10 = 20	3 x 10 = 30	4 x 10 = 40	5 x 10 = 50

6 x 1 = 6	7 x 1 = 7	8 x 1 = 8	9 x 1 = 9	10 x 1 = 10
6 x 2 = 12	7 x 2 = 14	8 x 2 = 16	9 x 2 = 18	10 x 2 = 20
6 x 3 = 18	7 x 3 = 21	8 x 3 = 24	9 x 3 = 27	10 x 3 = 30
6 x 4 = 24	7 x 4 = 28	8 x 4 = 32	9 x 4 = 36	10 x 4 = 40
6 x 5 = 30	7 x 5 = 35	8 x 5 = 40	9 x 5 = 45	10 x 5 = 50
6 x 6 = 36	7 x 6 = 42	8 x 6 = 48	9 x 6 = 54	10 x 6 = 60
6 x 7 = 42	7 x 7 = 49	8 x 7 = 56	9 x 7 = 63	10 x 7 = 70
6 x 8 = 48	7 x 8 = 56	8 x 8 = 64	9 x 8 = 72	10 x 8 = 80
6 x 9 = 54	7 x 9 = 63	8 x 9 = 72	9 x 9 = 81	10 x 9 = 90
6 x 10 = 60	7 x 10 = 70	8 x 10 = 80	9 x 10 = 90	10 x 10 = 100

Name: _____   Date: _____

Hamilton Troll meets
ELWOOD WOODPECKER

1. If Boswell Beaver uses 2 trees to make a dam, how many dams can he make if he has 10 trees?

_____ x _____ = _____

2. If Elwood Woodpecker eats seven bugs a day, how many will he eat in a week?

_____ x _____ = _____

3. If Hamilton Troll teaches three animals about petrified wood and they each teach three animals, how many animals will know about petrified wood?

_____ x _____ = _____

Name: _____   Date: _____

Hamilton Troll meets
ELWOOD WOODPECKER

1. Baxter and Boswell Beaver each cut down three logs. How many logs do they have total?

_____ X _____ = _____

2. Elwood Woodpecker has three butterflies land on his head. How many heads are there?

_____

X _____

= _____

3. How many flower petals are there in all? Fill in the blanks with the question and answer.

_____ X _____ = _____

Hamilton Troll Curriculum
www.HamiltonTrollBooks.com

SCIENCE PROJECTS

A Legend: "Why Beavers Build Dams"
Told to Hamilton Troll by Boswell & Baxter Beaver

When the first beavers walked the Earth, they lived on land. They gnawed on trees and built their dens, but the wolves would dig them out and the bears could break in.

So a wise She-Beaver sent her children forth to find a safe place to live. They searched the caves but the rocks hurt their feet. They searched the desert but there were no trees and the prickly plants hurt their tender mouths.

One day they happened upon a wide swift running stream; there they decided to rest. However, they were surrounded by their enemies! On one side of the stream there was a pack of wolves, on the other side were bears.

They leapt into the water and swam to the middle of the stream and there they were safe. The wolves and bears saw that they could not get near the beavers so they soon left.

Seeing how they had escaped their enemies the beavers decided that water may be a safe place to live, but how could they raise their cubs and where would they sleep?

Then the youngest beaver had an idea. With the trees they gnawed down and mud gathered and plastered on the trees, they could create their den on water. So they did.

We don't know if the story is true, but our Grand-Pappy told it to us when we were young cubs and now we have told it to you.

Written by: Leigh A. Klug

Definitions & Vocabulary Words:

Gnaw - to chew
Cubs - baby or young beavers
Plaster - to cover a surface with a thick layer of mud

BEAVER DAMS

The primary reason that beavers build dams is to create a safe place where they can build their homes. These homes called lodges are built in deep, still pools of water and have underwater entryways.

There are typically two dens within the lodge, one for drying off after exiting the water, and another, drier one, where the family actually lives.

Hamilton Troll meets
ELWOOD WOODPECKER

Beavers build dams in rivers and streams. These dams are their home. The dams also create homes for fish, frogs, turtles and other aquatic life.

Why do you think aquatic life likes to live around beaver dams?

What are three things you need to make a beaver dam?

_____ + _____ + _____ = **Beaver Dam**

Draw a beaver dam below.

Hamilton Troll meets
ELWOOD WOODPECKER

The tree Elwood Woodpecker was tapping on was as hard as stone. This is because it was petrified wood. This means it turned into stone. The tree fell, was buried by mud like what might happen after a flood. The wood rotted away and the mud hardened turning into stone, which looked like the wood.

Draw a three part diagram of how petrified wood is made.

Chatterton Squirrel is afraid of falling. This is because gravity would pull him down to the ground (fast).

**Science
Gravity**

Gravity is what keeps us from floating off into space.

Isaac Newton was the person who came up with the theory of gravity when an apple fell from a tree on his head.

Some of the things you can do to prove there is gravity are:

- Slide down a slide
- Hang on monkey bars

Jump up - what happens? _____

Throw a ball - what happens? _____

What else can you do? _____

_____

_____

_____

Name _____ Date _____

Science/Math
Gravity

Earths gravity is much stronger than the gravity on the moon. In fact, the moons gravity is **6** <u>times weaker</u> than Earth.

If you jump up from the ground on Earth you will instantly be pulled back to the ground. If you jump on the moon it will take a few moments before you land. Have you ever seen the astronauts walking on the moon video?

So how much would you weigh on the moon?
Answer the following questions to get your answer.

1. Weigh yourself using a regular bathroom scale. What is your weight? _____ lbs

2. Now divide that by the number 6

$$6\overline{)}$$

3. On the moon I would weigh: _____ lbs

Which came first, the dinosaur or the egg?

Just like birds, turtles and tadpoles; dinosaurs were born from eggs. Their mother laid the eggs, they grow inside and when they are big enough, they hatch, by poking themselves through the shell and greeting the world.

Some say the dinosaur came before the egg, the mother had to lay the egg. But where did the mother come from? An egg? She had to be born to grow up. So maybe the egg came first.

But if the egg came first, who kept it warm? And where did the egg come from originally?

This is called a paradox. It is a question without an answer. Which choice do you think makes the most sense. The dinosaur or the egg? Discuss your answer.

DINOSAURS

There are so many, let's just name a few.

Pterodactyl

Triceratops

Stegosaurus

Brontosaurus

DID YOU KNOW?

Dinosaurs

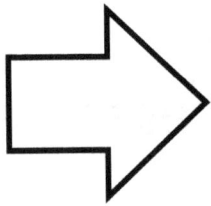

➡️ Dinosaurs lived 237 million years ago. They became extinct (all died out) 66 million years ago, so they lived on Earth for 171 million years.

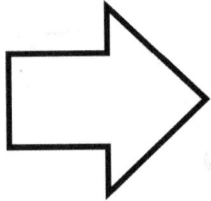

➡️ While dinosaurs became extinct, many species that lived along dinosaurs survived, like turtles, crocodiles, other reptiles, marine life and even birds

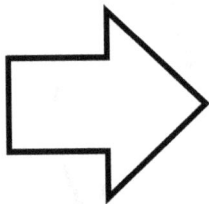

➡️ Dinosaurs were reptiles (cold-blooded) and laid eggs. Some dinosaurs were carnivorous (meat eaters) while others were herbivores (eating plants)

Dinosaurs

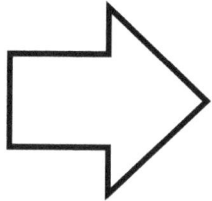

➡️ Some dinosaurs were as tall as a nine story building, and as long as two football fields (190 feet)

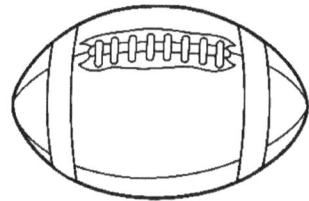

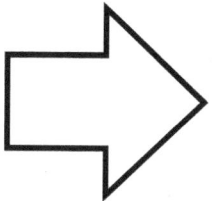

➡️ Some dinosaurs weighed 150 tons (300,000 pounds) while others barely weighed a pound.

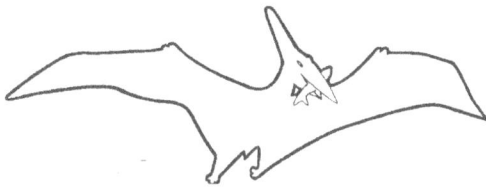

6 foot tall human

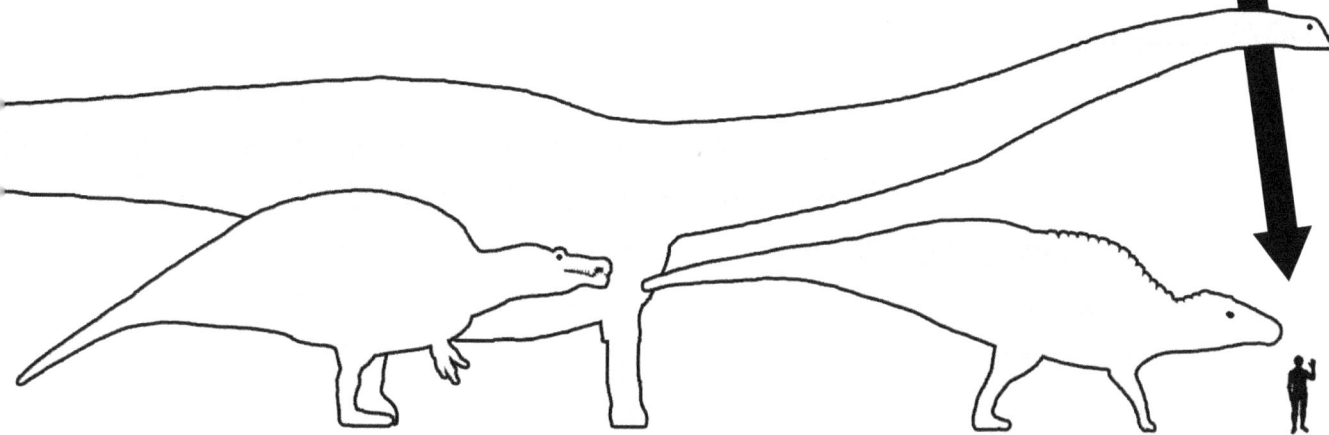

Life Cycles
science

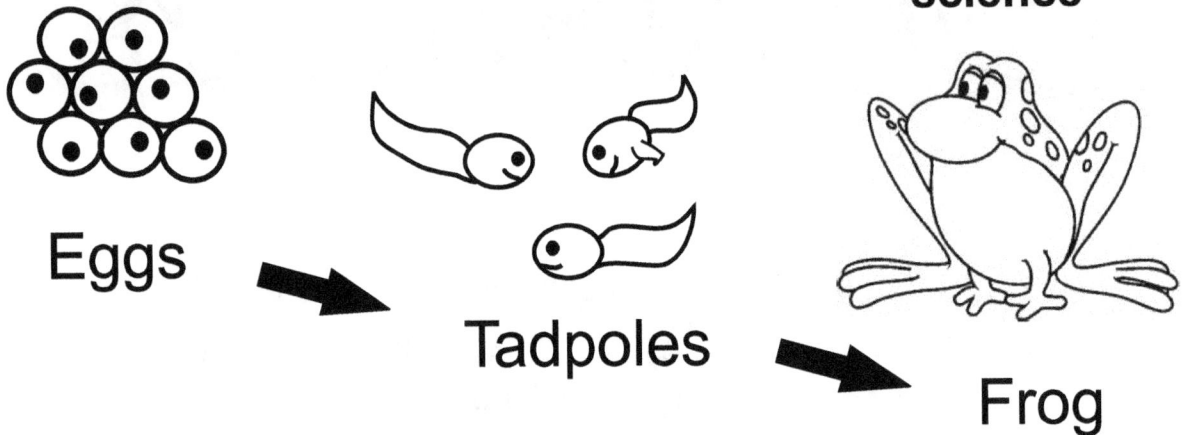

Eggs

Tadpoles

Frog

Frogs lay their eggs in the water. The floating clump of eggs is called 'frog spawn'. The cells inside the egg begins to grow.

In about 21 days tadpoles emerge from the eggs. They eat algae and plants for nutrients, continuing to grow. The tadpole has a long thick tail it uses to swim through the water.

In about 5 weeks the hind legs start to show and their tail starts to shrink. They shed their skin and grow lungs. When the tail is gone, the frog is ready to come out of the water and live on land.

Eventually, it will lay it's own set of eggs in the water and the life cycle will start again.

Name _____ Date _____

Caterpillar

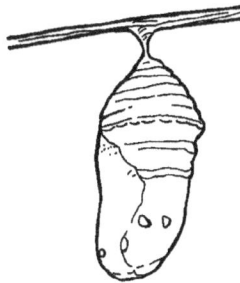

Cocoon

Butterfly

LOOK BUT DON'T TOUCH!!

Caterpillars look like worms with legs. They usually have stripes or an interesting pattern. They eat a lot of plants and leaves and so they grow very quickly. They also eat this much for when they are in the cocoon.

Once a butterfly creates and enters their cocoon, they may stay inside of it for many months. This is called the Chrysalis. They are transforming themselves into something amazing. Their bodies are changing. They are growing wings, and when they emerge they will not look anything like the caterpillar that went into the cocoon.

Once the butterfly is ready to emerge from the cocoon it will begin to SLOWLY emerge (3-4 hours). They are slow because their wings are very soft and fragile. If you try to help a butterfly in this stage you will stop its transformation and it will never fly.

Science
Water Cycle

The water cycle is made up of a 3 main parts:
- condensation
- evaporation
- precipitation

Condensation is when water vapor in the air gets cold and changes back into liquid, forming clouds.

Evaporation is when the sun heats up water in rivers, lakes or oceans and turns it into vapor or steam. The water vapor or steam leaves the river, lake or ocean and goes into the air.
Note: vapor is a word in e_vapor_ation.

Precipitation is rain. This occurs when so much water has collected in the sky that it cannot hold it anymore. The clouds get heavy and water falls back to the earth in the form of rain.

Science
Water Cycle
Projects

Condensation

Pour a glass of cold water on a hot day and watch what happens. You may even want to put a couple ice cubes in it.

Water forms on the outside of the glass.

That water didn't leak through the glass, it actually came from the air.

Water vapor in the warm air, turns back into liquid when it touches the cold glass.

Steam / Rain
With your parents help

Heat some water (it does not need to boil but should be hot). Pour it in a glass and then cover the top of the glass with syran wrap.

Wrap a rubber band around it to hold it tight. Watch what happens.

The heat evaporates the water converting it to vapor/steam.

That vapor collects on the wrap and when there is enough, it will rain back down into the glass, just like the water cycle on Earth!

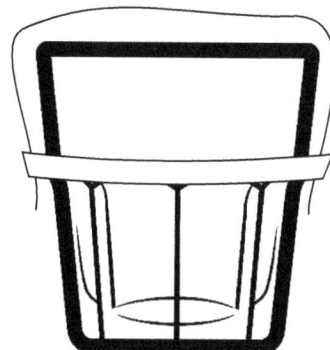

DID YOU KNOW?
BUMBLE BEES

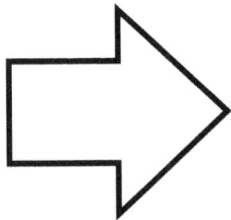

➡ Bumble Bees are color blind. They can't see the color RED.

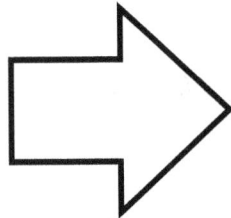

➡ Male drone bumble bees can't sting.

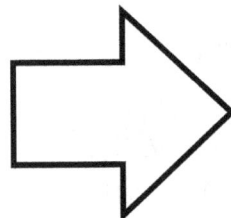

➡ Some Bumble bee's don't live in hives, most live in the ground.

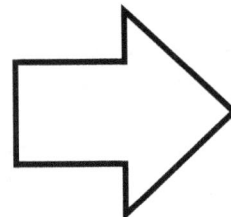

➡ They only make enough honey to feed themselves.

DID YOU KNOW?

WOODPECKERS

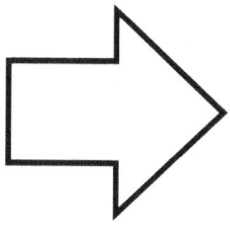

➡️ Woodpeckers tap holes in wood and trees, in hopes of finding bugs to eat but they also drink tree sap and eat fruits, nuts and seeds.

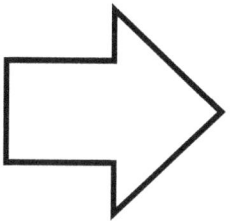

➡️ Woodpecker feet have toes that face front AND back so they can grip hold of anything (tree or pole).

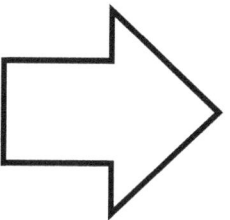

➡️ Woodpeckers don't sing but they are really good drummers! They communicate by tapping (on anything) so if you ever see a woodpecker drumming on something like a metal pole or trash can, they're not trying to find food, but trying to talk to another woodpecker.

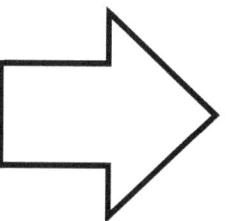

➡️ Woodpeckers can peck up to 20 times per second!

DID YOU KNOW?
ARMADILLOs

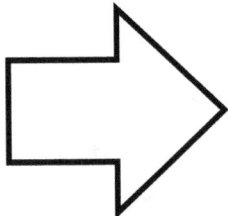

→ Armadillos are the only living mammals with armor-like shells.

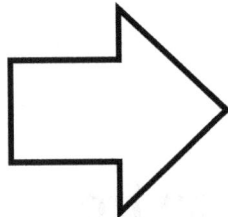

→ Armadillos are born as identical quadruplets (meaning 4 exact copies).

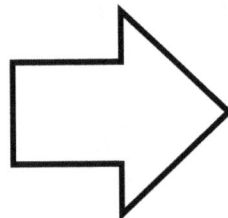

→ Armadillos have poor vision, but they have a strong sense of smell. They can smell up to 7 inches below the ground!

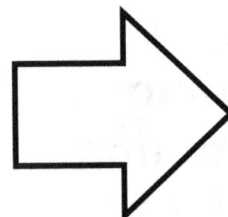

→ Armadillos sleep for 18-19 hours a day and are active during the night.

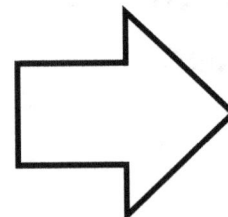

→ Some armadillos have the ability to roll into a ball when they sense danger, but not all can.

DID YOU KNOW?
OWLS

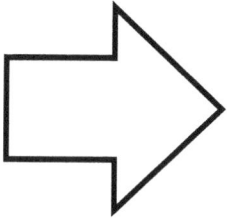

→ Owls cannot chew their food because they do not have teeth. Instead, they swallow their food whole.

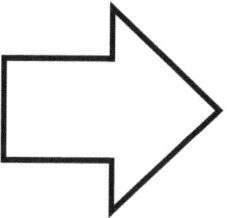

→ When their food contains things they can't digest, they regurgitate pellets (throw-up).

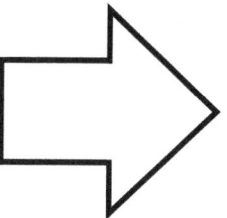

→ Owls are unable to move their eyes which means they must turn their entire head to see in a different direction.

DID YOU KNOW?
BEAVERS

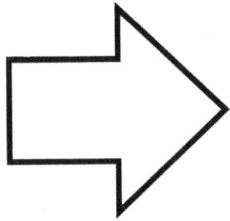

➡️ **A beaver is semi-aquatic, meaning they live in the water but can walk on land.**

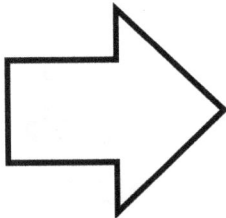

➡️ **Beavers have thick fur and webbed feet (like a duck) for swimming.**

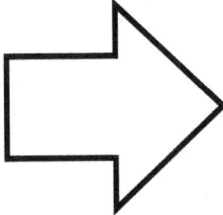

➡️ **Beavers have large flat tails they use as paddles and for packing mud on the dams.**

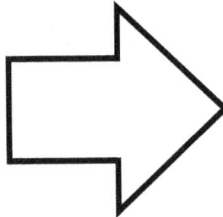

➡️ **Beavers have sharp teeth for gnawing on wood, that grow back like fingernails.**

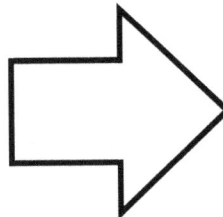

➡️ **Beavers are herbivores, they eat wood and plants; like water lilies.**

DID YOU KNOW?
BEAVER DAMS

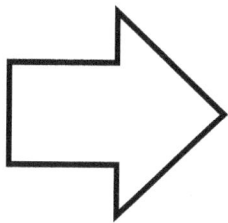

There is a theory that beavers build dams to silence the rushing water sound, which makes their homes quieter but also provides the ability to hear any approaching predators so they can dive below the water for protection.

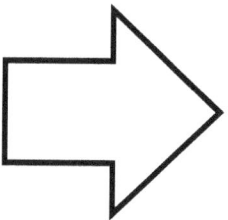

Beaver dams have a profound effect on ecosystems, by creating wetlands; lush environments which attract fish, ducks, frogs and other creatures.

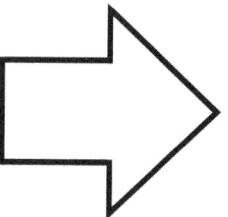

The largest beaver dam was over 2,780 feet long (850 meters) in Wood Buffalo National Park in Alberta, Canada.

DID YOU KNOW?
FROGS

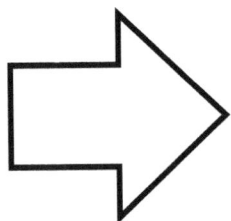

➡ Frogs don't drink; they absorb water through their skin.

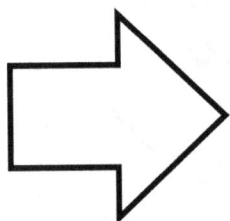

➡ The smallest known frog is about ½ inch long, and the largest known frog is about a foot long.

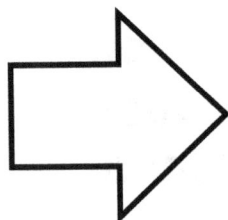

➡ There are over 4,000 frog species in the world, with only 88 of them in the United States.

DID YOU KNOW?
RACCOONS

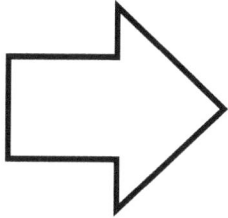

→ Raccoons climb trees when they feel threatened. They also make their homes in old tree hollows (holes).

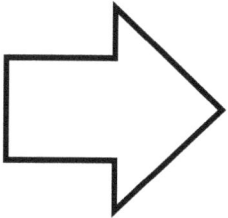

→ Raccoons have been known to clean their food.

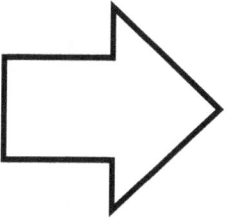

→ They are very smart at solving problems and have been known to remember solutions for up to three years.

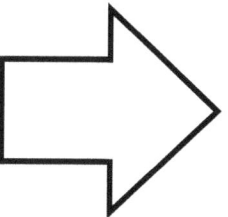

→ They do not wear masks but their eyes are surrounded by brown/black fur.

DID YOU KNOW?

Butterflies

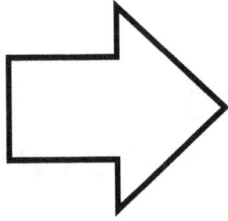

→ Butterflies have lived on Earth about 50 million years.

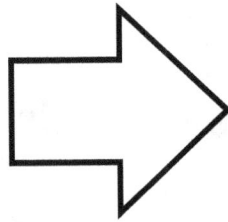

→ They have four large brightly colored wings that are made of soft scales.

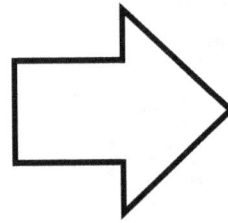

→ Butterflies start out as caterpillars that eat leaves until they go into their cocoon and emerge later as a butterfly.

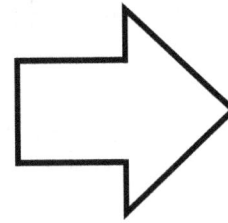

→ Butterflies eat nectar and pollen from flowers, along with tree sap and rotting fruit.

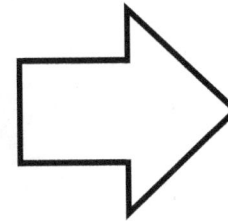

→ Butterflies migrate (travel) as much as 3000 miles per year.

→ There are about 20,000 species (types) of butterflies in the world!

DID YOU KNOW?
Mushroom

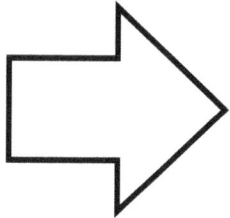

➤ Mushrooms are also called toadstools.

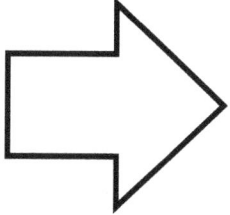

➤ Some mushrooms seem to appear overnight, although it takes them a couple days to appear.

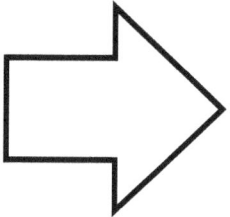

➤ A mushroom is a fungi (type of fungus) not to be confused with being a 'fun guy'.

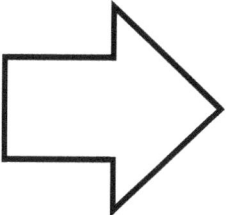

➤ There are over 5000 types of mushrooms of different shapes, colors and sizes. Some can be eaten, some can not.

NEVER
EAT A WILD
MUSHROOM!!!

BATS

DID YOU KNOW?

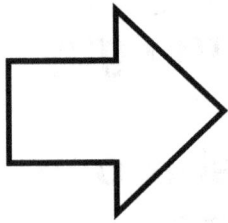

➡ Bats are nocturnal, meaning they mostly come out at night.

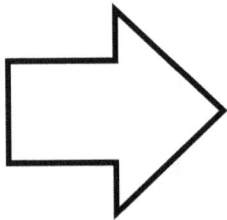

➡ Bats are the only mammals that can truly fly. A mammal is a warm-blooded animal. Birds are not mammals.

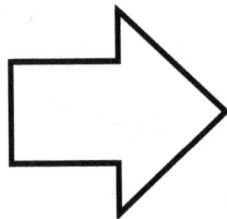

➡ Bats use Echolocation to fly. They use a series of beeps that echo off the walls and bounce back at them to "see" where to go. Most bats are blind.

➡ There are 1100 species (types) of bats in the world. Some can be as small as 1 inch or as big as 5 feet long.

FUN
STUFF

Hamilton Troll loves watching the ants work.

He wishes he could see the tunnels within an ant pile and go inside and explore. But what if he got lost? Help this ant get through the maze by going under and over in the tunnels to get

Start

End

Did you know that trees have rings?

Not like gold rings, but lines that look like circles. These circles are called rings, like you see below, and if you count the rings, you will know how many years that tree had been alive.

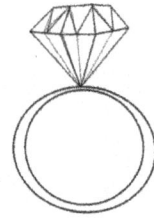

Make your way through this tree stumps rings to get to the center .

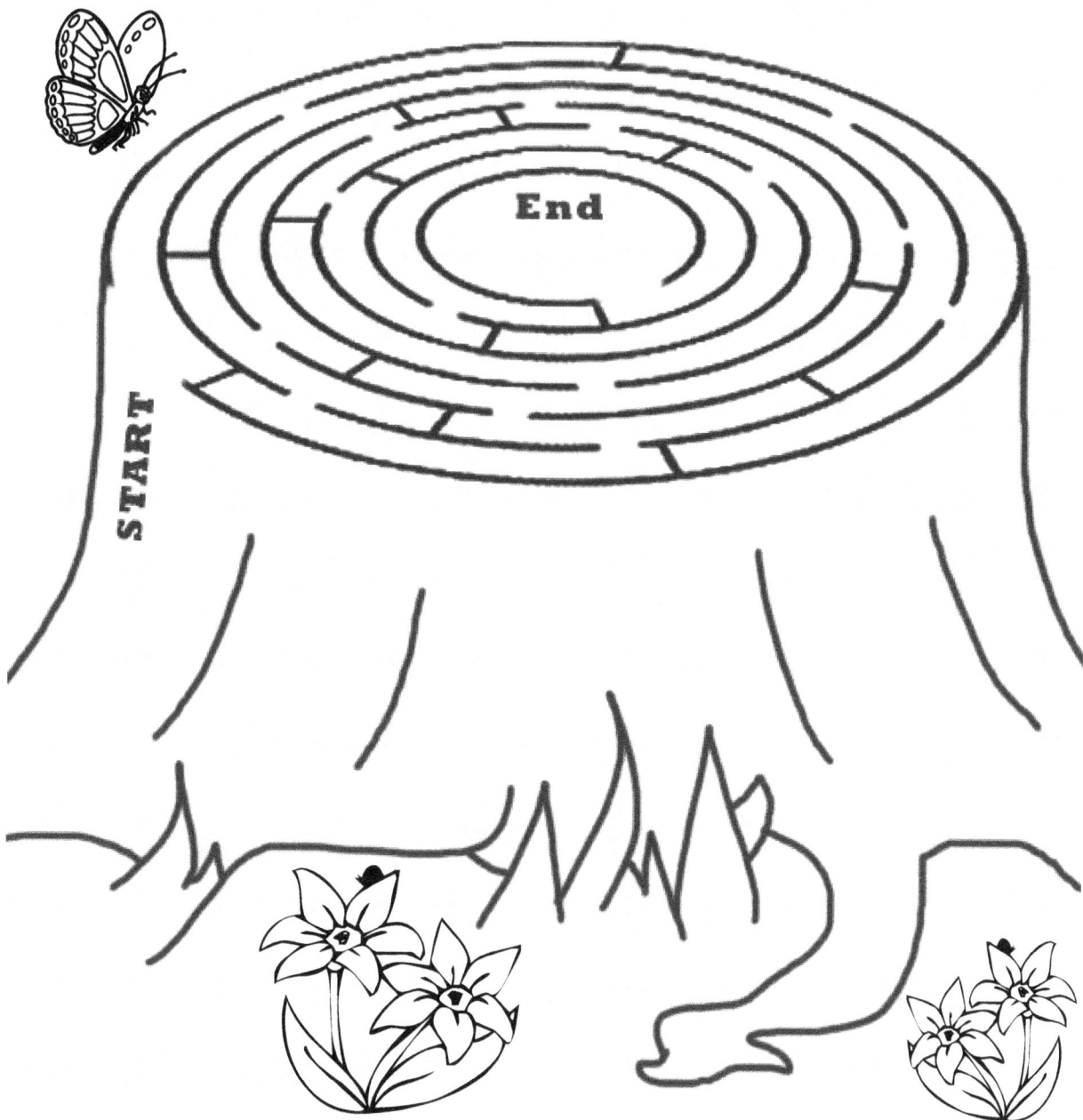

START

End

When the Wind Blows...

it makes it difficult for birds to fly. They get caught in wind currents which spiral them around. Help this bird make it through the wind currents to get to the other side.

Finish

Start

Trolls are usually hard to find.

But in this word search they are very easy.
How many times can you find the
word TROLL in this search?

T	R	O	L	L	O	R	T	R	L
R	R	T	R	O	L	L	R	L	L
O	T	O	L	L	R	R	O	T	O
L	L	O	R	T	T	O	L	L	R
L	L	O	R	L	R	O	L	T	T
R	L	T	O	L	L	O	T	R	O
T	R	O	L	O	L	L	O	R	T
R	L	R	R	R	O	L	T	L	O
O	L	L	O	T	L	L	O	O	L
L	O	L	T	L	L	O	R	T	R
L	R	O	R	O	R	R	O	R	O
R	T	R	R	O	T	T	L	R	L
O	R	T	R	O	L	L	O	R	T

How many
times did
you find
the word
TROLL?

_____

Pink Light Sprite

Will always be around but will be out of sight... which makes her hard to find. But in this word search you can find the word SPRITE a whole lot of times!

Haw many times can you find SPRITE?

E	T	I	R	P	S	P	R	I	T	E
E	S	T	S	P	R	I	T	E	S	R
S	S	P	R	I	T	E	S	R	S	P
E	T	I	R	P	S	S	P	R	P	S
E	T	I	R	P	S	P	R	S	R	E
E	S	P	R	I	E	I	I	S	I	T
T	T	S	P	R	T	E	T	R	T	I
I	S	I	T	E	I	R	E	P	E	R
R	P	S	R	S	R	R	I	T	E	P
P	R	I	T	P	P	T	R	I	P	S
S	P	R	I	T	S	P	R	I	T	E
P	R	I	S	P	R	I	T	E	T	R

WORD SEARCH

S	Q	U	I	R	R	E	L	K	T
K	K	O	W	L	A	E	E	C	H
E	N	U	T	R	L	L	S	I	G
E	L	O	N	U	T	O	P	T	I
T	R	O	L	K	T	I	R	S	L
E	L	W	O	O	D	P	I	T	K
R	C	H	A	M	I	L	T	O	N
B	A	R	N	E	Y	B	E	E	I
R	E	K	A	T	I	H	W	O	P
C	H	A	T	T	E	R	T	O	N

HAMILTON   CHATTERTON
TROLL   SQUIRREL
PINK LIGHT   WHITAKER
SPRITE   OWL
SKEETER   ELWOOD
SKUNK   STICK
BARNEY BEE   NUT

N	A	N	O	T	R	E	C	H	A	T	N
C	A	T	O	O	N	C	H	A	R	O	O
T	H	R	E	N	C	A	R	T	T	N	T
R	H	E	T	R	T	O	O	R	O	C	R
E	R	T	R	E	H	O	E	A	N	H	E
T	H	T	E	T	R	T	N	H	T	A	T
A	T	T	A	T	T	T	H	C	E	T	A
H	A	A	R	A	T	R	O	N	R	T	A
C	R	H	H	C	H	A	T	T	R	O	H
T	A	C	H	A	T	E	R	T	O	N	C

There is only one Chatterton Squirrel just like there is only one of you!

So this word search puzzle is a little different. The name Chatterton can only be found one time in the entire puzzle!

Can you find it?

CHATTERTON

1

There are now **7** books of the Hamilton Troll series *(and many more to come)*.
In celebration of seven books you must find Hamilton's name in this search **7** times!

HAMILTON

L	I	T	O	N	O	T	L	I	M	A	H
H	A	H	A	M	I	L	T	O	N	O	N
N	A	N	H	A	M	I	N	L	O	T	A
O	M	M	A	H	A	M	I	L	T	O	N
T	I	L	I	H	T	H	A	M	L	T	N
L	L	O	T	L	I	M	A	H	I	T	H
I	I	N	I	N	T	H	A	M	M	N	A
M	M	M	A	H	N	O	T	I	A	O	M
A	A	M	I	L	T	O	N	L	H	T	I
H	H	O	N	O	T	L	I	M	A	H	L

Hamilton Troll Curriculum
www.HamiltonTrollBooks.com

READING

COMPREHENSION

QUIZ

ANSWERS

Hamilton Troll meets
Pink Light Sprite

Quiz

1) Where does Hamilton Troll live?
 a) tree
 b) shoe
 c) hole
 d) box

2) What is Hamilton Troll afraid of?
 a) loud thunder
 b) rain flooding his home
 c) bright lightning
 d) strong wind

3) Where does Hamilton Troll go for safety?
 a) Hide Away Flop
 b) big leaf plants
 c) elephant ear leaves
 d) all of the above

4) Why can Hamilton Troll see Pink Light Sprite
 a) her wings got wet and she couldn't fly
 b) she was resting from a long trip
 c) she wanted to make a new friend
 d) she wanted to be alone

5) What does Pink Light Sprite suggest Hamilton Troll do?
 a) move to a new location
 b) don't worry about the rain
 c) transplant the leaves near his home
 d) use a mushroom as a door

Name: _____   Date: _____

Hamilton Troll meets Skeeter Skunk

Quiz

1) What does Skeeter Skunk want to do?
 a) Eat flowers
 b) Spray everyone he can
 c) Watch the big game
 (d) Play in the stick nut game

2) What did the friends NOT try to solve Skeeter Skunk's problem?
 a) Cover his eyes
 b) Cover his smell
 c) Cover his ears
 (d) Cover his mouth

3) Why did they cover Skeeter Skunk with flowers?
 a) They were trying to make him look pretty
 b) They wanted to play dress-up
 (c) They were trying to cover the smell of his spray
 d) They wanted to hide him in the flowers

4) What did the shy bunny say?
 (a) When I eat these red berries I become a real stinker.
 b) I get shy around others and my cheeks turn red.
 c) I was so embarrassed I ran off to hide.
 d) Whenever I play stick-nut I get afraid.

5) In the end, what was it that kept Skeeter from spraying everyone?
 a) He was out of spray
 b) He was tired
 (c) He had made friends
 d) He didn't want to spray them

Name: _____   Date: _____

Hamilton Troll meets
Barney Bee

Quiz

1) What was Barney Bee doing when Hamilton Troll found him?
 a) Flying around
 b) Buzzing a neat song
 c) Eating pollen from a flower
 d) Playing with other bees

2) Why did Barney Bee fly past the red flowers?
 a) Because he wanted to get to the other side
 b) Because they didn't smell good
 c) Because bees are color blind and he didn't see them
 d) Because the pink ones taste much better

3) What does Barney Bee say to explain why he doesn't have friends?
 a) All the bees are to busy
 b) All the birds are to fast
 c) All the critters are afraid to get stung
 d) All of the above

4) Why did Barney Bee fall out of the sky?
 a) His wings were tired
 b) His wings couldn't hold his weight
 c) The wind pushed him down
 d) There was a nice flower on the ground

5) What does Barney need to do to keep flying?
 a) Eat less pollen
 b) Exercise
 c) Play
 d) All of the above

Name: _____ Date: _____

Hamilton Troll meets
Chatterton Squirrel

Quiz

1) What were Chatterton Squirrel's parents teaching him?
  a) How to fly
  b) How to run across tree limbs
  (c) How to leap from one tree to the next
  d) How to talk like a squirrel

2) Who went first to show how it was done?
  a) Mother
  (b) Father
  c) Brother
  d) Sister

3) Why wouldn't Chatterton do this task?
  (a) He was afraid of falling
  b) He didn't feel like it
  c) He didn't need to
  d) He already knew how to

4) What did Hamilton sit on to watch the squirrels practice?
  a) A red rock
  b) A small log
  c) A green clover
  (d) A crimson clover

5) What did Hamilton Troll do to help Chatterton learn?
  a) Draw a line in the dirt
  b) Make big purple X's on the ground
  c) Suggest Chatterton practice on the ground first
  (d) All of the above

Hamilton Troll meets
ELWOOD WOODPECKER

Quiz

1) What gave Elwood Woodpecker the headache?
 (a) Pecking on petrified wood
 b) Playing too many video games
 c) He got hit on the head
 d) None of the above

2) Who did Hamilton and Elwood visit to learn about petrified wood?
 a) Rachel Raccoon
 b) Pink Light Sprite
 (c) Beaver Brothers
 d) Skeeter Skunk

3) How did the petrified wood get there?
 (a) Floated down the river
 b) Dropped off a tree
 c) Rolled down a hill
 d) All of the above

4) What happened to Boswell Beaver when he first learned about petrified wood?
 a) He tripped over it and hurt his foot
 b) He made it into a beaver dam
 c) He ran off to find out more about it
 (d) He chipped his front tooth on it

5) What does Hamilton Troll do now that he knows what petrified wood is?
 a) He keeps it to himself
 b) He hangs out with the beaver brothers and goes swimming
 (c) He tells the others about what he learned
 d) He spends the rest of the day with Elwood Woodpecker

Name: _____   Date: _____

Hamilton Troll meets DINOSAURS

Quiz

1) What did Hamilton Troll find that led him on this journey?
 a) A rock shaped like a dinosaur
 (b) A fossil that looked like a seashell
 c) A rock that looked like a flower
 d) A fossil shaped like a mouse

2) Where did the beaver brothers
   take Hamilton Troll?
 a) A school
 (b) A museum
 c) A computer
 d) A library

3) How did Hamilton Troll find
   himself in dinosaur time?
 a) A time machine
 b) A magic door
 c) A river ride
 (d) A dream

4) How big were the footprints?
 a) Twice as big as Hamilton
 b) As tall as a tree
 c) Ten times longer than him
 (d) Five times his length, six, maybe eight

5) What did the mama dinosaur teach Hamilton Troll?
 a) Dinosaurs are all friendly
 b) All dinosaurs eat plants
 (c) There are plant eaters and meat eaters
 d) She rules the land

Hamilton
Troll meets
Whitaker Owl

1) What are Whitaker Owl's parents teaching him?
 a) How to fly
 (b) How to hoot
 c) How to catch food
 d) None of the above

2) What does Hamilton Troll think Whitaker sounds like?
 a) A bear
 b) An Owl
 c) A cat
 (d) A ghost

3) What happens that upsets everyone?
 (a) A bear comes near
 b) A ghost appears
 c) His parents fly away
 d) A bat flies by

4) What did the bear say?
 a) Do you taste like chicken?
 b) You sound like a ghost.
 (c) These woods are haunted.
 d) Can we play together?

5) What does Whitaker do to save the night?
 (a) He flies by the bear hooting like a ghost
 b) He asks a couple ghosts to scare the bear away
 c) He asks his parents for help
 d) He screams out loud

Name: _____   Date: _____

Hamilton Troll meets
RUDY RAT

Quiz

1) Why is Rosa Raccoon crying?
 a) she lost the Stick-Nut game
 b) Rudy Rat fell and hurt himself
 c) she was lost and couldn't get home
 (d) Rudy Rat was being mean

2) What did Rudy Rat do?
 a) he took Susie's flower
 b) he ate Billy's lunch
 c) he tripped little Tim in the hall
 (d) all of the above

3) What does Hamilton want to do about Rudy Rat?
 a) punish him
 (b) talk to him
 c) be mean to him
 d) none of the above

4) What do the kids do to Rudy Rat?
 a) bully him back
 b) make him run away
 (c) invite him to play
 d) scare him and laugh

5) What does PAWS stand for?
 a) Prepare, Answer, Write, Spell
 b) Pretend, Approach, Welcome, Smile
 (c) Pause, Approach, Welcome, Smile
 d) Pause, Answer, Welcome, Sing

Hamilton Troll

and the Case of the

Missing Home

1) What scares Hamilton out of his home?
  a) a bear growling
  (b) a loud sound
  c) a screaming cat
  d) a clap of thunder

2) What happened to his tree?
  a) it fell down
  (b) it was cut down
  c) it disappeared like magic
  d) none of the above

3) What does Rachel Raccoon find out?
  a) the tree is gone forever
  b) it was taken to a human's home
  c) it is going to be used for Christmas
  (d) all of the above

4) What does Hamilton Troll want to do?
  a) go find a new home
  b) run off and cry
  c) tell everyone about it
  (d) go visit his tree

5) What was the tree used for?
  a) making furniture
  b) building a beaver dam
  (c) decoration for Christmas
  d) firewood

Name: _____ Date: _____

Hamilton Troll meets
FIONA THE DOG

Quiz

1) What items are going missing?
 a) Rudy Rat's hat
 b) Merle Mouse's mat
 c) Amara's broom
 (d) all of the above

2) How did Rudy Rat feel about his missing hat?
 a) very sad
 b) confused
 (c) angry
 d) lonely

3) What happens to Hamilton Troll?
 a) his ladder goes missing
 b) he gets carried away
 c) he meets Fiona the dog
 (d) all of the above

4) What does Hamilton Troll discover?
 a) all of the items were taken by the wind
 b) everyone's things were broken
 (c) Fiona took everyone's things
 d) everyone misplaced their stuff

5) What does Hamilton do to solve this?
 a) He tells Fiona she is bad
 b) He tells everyone what Fiona did
 c) He takes his ladder home
 (d) He suggests Fiona return the stuff

Name: _____ Date: _____

Hamilton Troll meets
Starlit Troll

Quiz

1) How did Starlit Troll arrive?
 a) She floated down the river
 b) She rode on a dog
 c) She rode on a duck
 d) She floated on the wind

2) What is special troll sight?
 a) being able to see magic
 b) being able to see other trolls
 c) being able to see fairies
 d) all of the above

3) What does Hamilton plan for the day?
 a) a hike
 b) a picnic
 c) a concert
 d) a party

4) Why couldn't he find Starlit?
 a) She had been everywhere he went
 b) She was looking for him
 c) He wasn't where she was looking
 d) All of the above

5) What did Hamilton do when he found everyone had eaten his food?
 a) He filled with defeat
 b) He huffed at everyone
 c) He realized everyone thought they were invited.
 d) All of the above

Name: _____   Date: _____

Hamilton Troll
and the
BIG RACE

1) Why did Starlit Troll get mad?
  a) Hamilton said she was fat.
  b) Hamilton didn't believe her.
  c) She was stung by a bee.
  d) She wanted to fly.

2) Who taught Hamilton about tree jumping?
  a) Beni Bunny
  b) Merle Mouse
  c) Chatterton Squirrel
  d) all of the above

3) What did Starlit do in the water?
  a) Swim
  b) Ski
  c) Skip
  d) Surf

4) Why did Hamilton lose?
  a) He was too slow.
  b) He tripped over a rock.
  c) Starlit knocked him over.
  d) None of the above.

5) What did Pink Light Sprite tell Hamilton?
  a) Are you going to sit here all by yourself?
  b) Are you going to waste every day?
  c) Are you too proud to congratulate her?.
  d) All of the above

Hamilton Troll Curriculum
www.HamiltonTrollBooks.com

LANGUAGE ARTS WORKSHEET

ANSWERS

WORD SCRAMBLE

The letters on the left will fill in the spots on the right. Use the word bank at the bottom for help.

KNIP TILGH TEPRIS   P I N K   L I G H T   S P R I T E

YEBRAN EBE   B A R N E Y   B E E

AAARM LODIMRALA   A M A R A   A R M A D I L L O

RKWTIAHE LOW   W H I T A K E R   O W L

ELRME SOUME   M E R L E   M O U S E

DELOOW   E L W O O D

REKETSE KKSUN   S K E E T E R   S K U N K

NILTAHOM LORTL   H A M I L T O N   T R O L L

RTTTEOACNH   C H A T T E R T O N

WORD BANK

AMARA ARMADILLO	BARNEY BEE
CHATTERTON	ELWOOD
HAMILTON TROLL	MERLE MOUSE
SKEETER SKUNK	WHITAKER OWL
PINK LIGHT SPRITE	

Name: _____ Date: _____

Hamilton Troll meets
Barney Bee

A noun is a word that names a person, place or thing. Cross off all the words on Barney Bee that are not nouns. Then write the nouns in the spaces below.

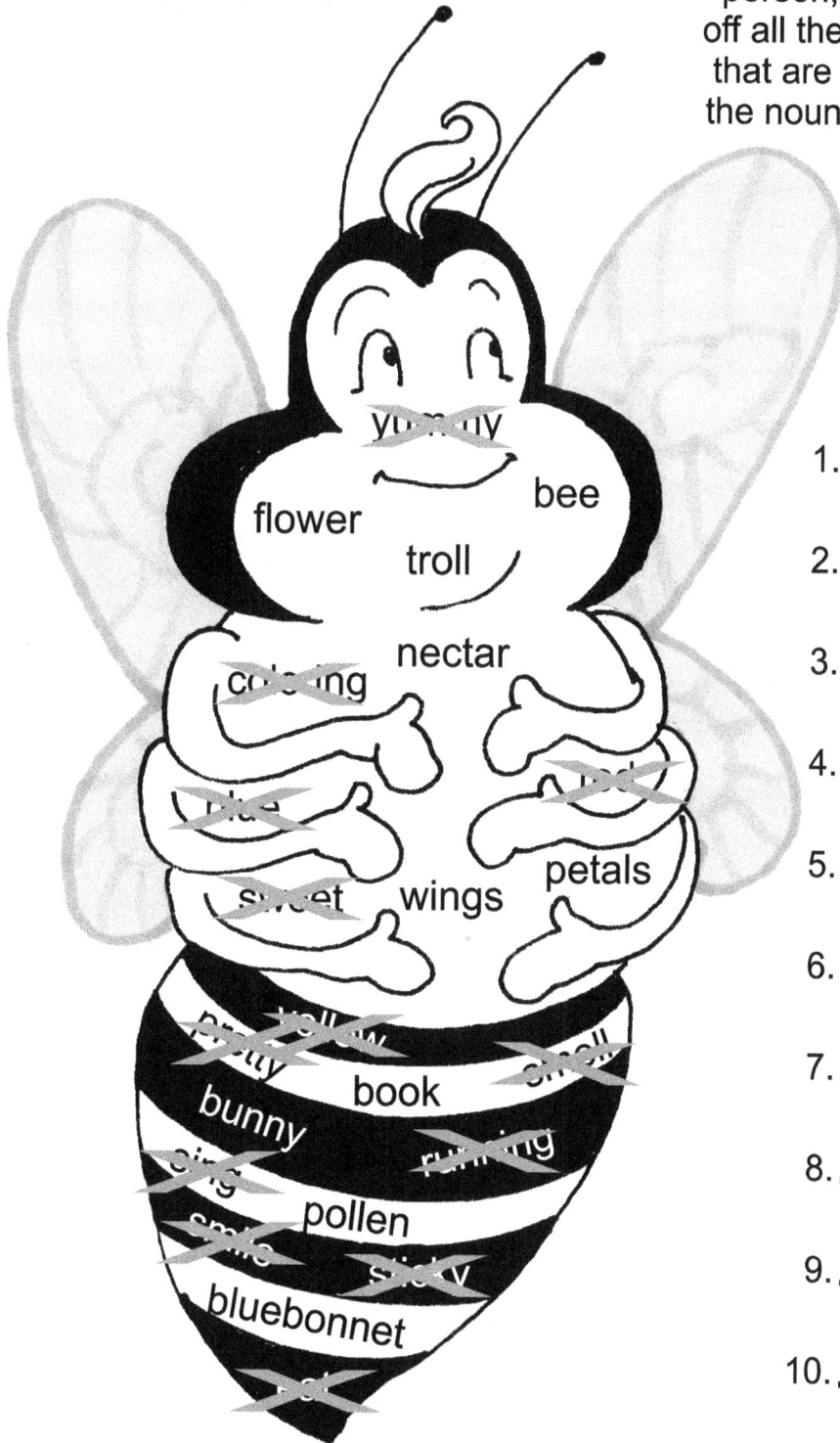

yummy
flower
bee
troll
nectar
coloring
blue
wings
sweet
petals
yellow
pretty
book
smell
bunny
sing
running
pollen
smile
sticky
bluebonnet

1. flower
2. bee
3. troll
4. nectar
5. wings
6. petals
7. book
8. bunny
9. pollen
10. bluebonnet

Name: _____ Date: _____

Hamilton Troll meets
Barney Bee

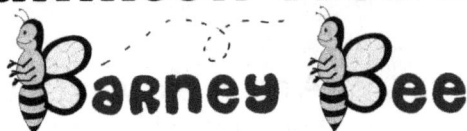

Verbs

**A verb is a word
that shows action.**

Circle the verb that correctly completes each sentence.

1. Hamilton Troll (dreams) about having wings.

2. Hamilton (tells) Barney to exercise.

3. Barney (runs) and (jumps) each day.

4. Barney Bee (falls) out of the sky.

5. Barney (skips) over the red flowers.

Fill in the blank with the verb that best works in the sentence.

1. Barney Bee _____**flies**_____ to each flower.
   flies, runs

2. Hamilton Troll _____**talks**_____ with Barney.
   talks, plays

3. Barney _____**eats**_____ nectar.
   breathes, eats

4. Hamilton _____**plays**_____ with his friends.
   plays, sings

5. Barney _____**rests**_____ on a flower.
   rests, jumps

Name: _____ Date: _____

Hamilton Troll meets
Pink Light Sprite

Adjectives

Circle the adjective in each sentence.
Underline the noun it describes.

1. Hamilton Troll has (red) hair.

2. Hamilton Troll has (brown) eyes.

3. Pink Light Sprite has (blonde) hair.

4. Pink Light Spite had (wet) wings.

5. Hamilton moved (big) plants.

6. Hamilton's home filled with (blue) rain water.

7. Hamilton hid under (big green) leaves.

Tips to Remember:

An **adjective** is a word that describes a noun.

An **adjective** can come before the noun it describes.

A **noun** is a person, place or thing.

Name: _____ Date: _____

Hamilton Troll meets *Skeeter Skunk*

Noun, Verb or Adjective

In the blanks write whether the underlined word is a noun, verb or adjective.

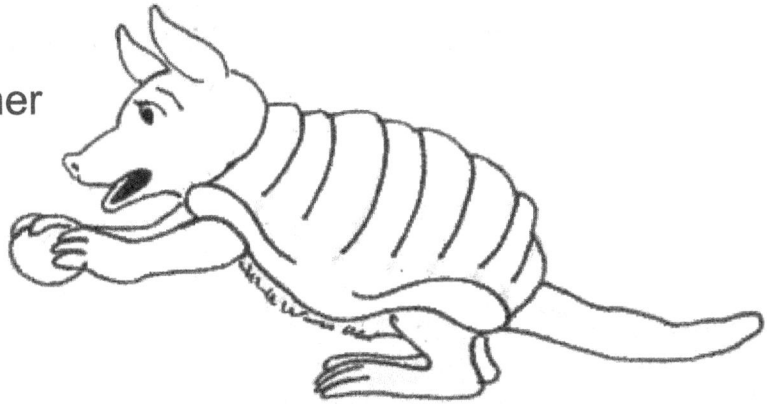

1. Amara Armadillo is a <u>catcher</u>. _____ noun _____

2. The nut, in Stick-Nut, is a <u>hazelnut</u>. _____ noun _____

3. The crowd <u>cheered</u> for Skeeter. _____ verb _____

4. Skeeter Skunk was <u>afraid</u> of the nut. _____ adjective _____

5. Hamilton Troll <u>helped</u> Skeeter. _____ verb _____

6. Amara Armadillo is <u>grey</u>. _____ adjective _____

7. Skeeter Skunk's spray is <u>stinky</u>. _____ adjective _____

8. A hazel nut is <u>yummy</u> to eat. _____ adjective _____

9. Skeeter <u>ran</u> as fast as a could. _____ verb _____

10. Skeeter Skunk ate <u>flowers</u>. _____ noun _____

Name _____ Date _____

In the blanks, write whether the underlined word is a noun, verb or adjective.

Noun, Verb or Adjective

1. Hamilton Troll lives in a hole. _____noun_____

2. Diggory Armadillo has a hard shell. _____adjective_____

3. Skeeter Skunk eats flowers. _____verb_____

4. Chatterton is a squirrel. _____noun_____

5. Chatterton Squirrel jumps in the trees. _____verb_____

6. Skeeter is a stinky skunk. _____adjective_____

7. Hamilton is a friendly troll. _____adjective_____

8. Five animals above have a tail. _____noun_____

9. Everyone sits down. _____verb_____

10. Hamilton is a green troll. _____adjective_____

Hamilton Troll
meet
FIONA THE DOG

Circle the adjectives and cross out the nouns.

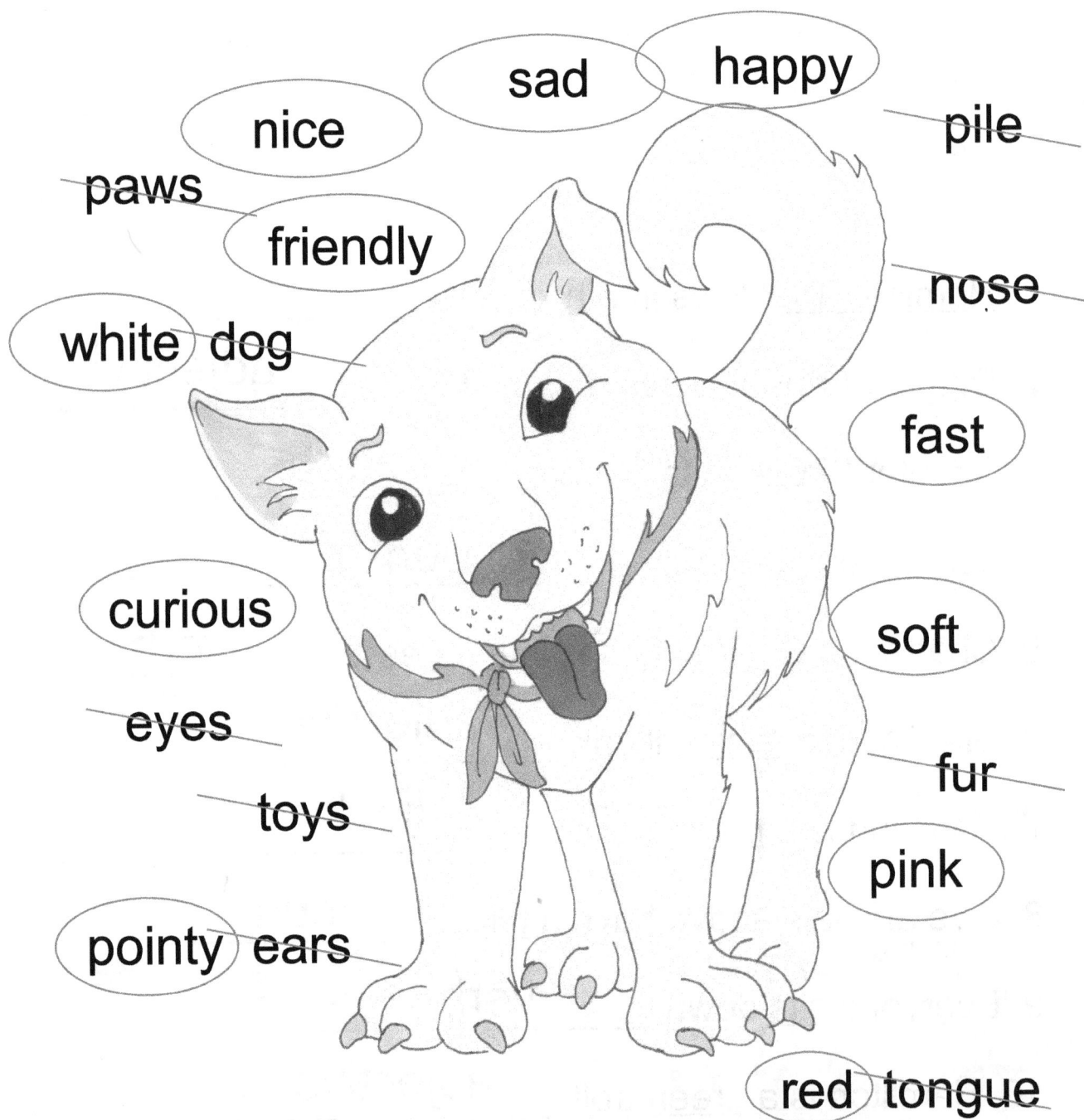

sad

happy

nice

~~pile~~

~~paws~~

friendly

~~nose~~

white ~~dog~~

fast

curious

soft

~~eyes~~

~~fur~~

~~toys~~

pink

pointy ~~ears~~

red ~~tongue~~

Name: _____ Date: _____

Hamilton Troll meets

Barney Bee

Homophone

Homophones are words that sound alike but have different spellings and meanings.

An example would be; two, to, too and there, they're, their.

You can have **two** apples.

You can go **to** school.

You can do your homework **too**.

You can go **there**.

It is **their** idea.

They're going to go sing.

Fill in the blanks with the correct homophone to the right.

1. Out of __**eight**__ flowers, Barney __**ate**__ two. | ate, eight

2. Barney said, "__**I**__ have pollen in my __**eyes**__. | I, eyes

3. "Do you __**know**__ why I can't fly?" Hamilton says, "__**no**__." | no, know

4. The wind __**blew**__ Barney by a __**blue**__ colored flower. | blue, blew

5. There were many __**rows**__ or flowers but only one red __**rose**__. | rose, rows

6. "I can't __**wait**__ to see if Barney lost __**weight**__." | wait, weight

7. There were a __**sea**__ of blue flowers as far as he could __**see**__. | see, sea

8. Barney __**flew**__ to a flower then sneezed like he had the __**flu**__. | flu, flew

9. Hamilton said, "I __**knew**__ you were __**new**__ to the area." | new, knew

10. With __**one**__ more player, the group __**won**__ the Stick-Nut game. | won, one

Name: _____   Date: _____

Hamilton Troll meets Skeeter Skunk

Read each sentence. Write the correct word on the line.

1. Skeeter Skunk wanted to _____play_____ the game.
   say   way   play

2. They tried to hide the smell with _____flowers_____.
   showers   flowers   powers

3. Skeeter Skunk is black and _____white_____.
   white   right   light

4. They covered his _____ears_____ and said boo.
   ears   fears   cheers

5. Hamilton and Skeeter _____won_____ the game.
   one   won   fun

Name _____ Date _____

Hamilton Troll meet *FIONA THE DOG*

Fill in the blanks with the word that best fits the sentence.

1. In the story, Fiona _____ **takes** _____ Rudy Rat's hat.
takes, breaks

2. Fiona the _____ **dog** _____ has white fur.
cat, dog

3. Fiona's favorite word is: _____ **Mine!** _____
Mine! , Yours.

4. Hamilton _____ **stands** _____ on a toy fire truck.
jumps, stands

5. Fiona _____ **hears** _____ her family.
hears, ignores

6. Fiona _____ **licks** _____ Hamilton Troll.
bites, licks

7. Hamilton and Fiona _____ **return** _____ the items.
keep, return

8. Fiona put everything she took into a _____ **pile** _____ .
hole, pile

9. Hamilton _____ **rides** _____ on Fiona's back.
rides, dances

10. Fiona wears a _____ **pink** _____ bandana around her neck.
blue, pink

Name: _____   Date: _____

Hamilton Troll is playing detective.

Help Hamilton Troll find the word that don't belong. Draw an **X** on the words in each group that do not match the word at the top.

Hamilton Troll lives in a hole.

live

~~jive~~ live
~~hive~~ ~~love~~

Hamilton walks along the path.

walk

~~wakl~~ ~~wolk~~
walk ~~welk~~

After it stopped raining, he came out.

after

~~ofter~~ after
~~alter~~ ~~often~~

There were two rainbows.

were

~~week~~ ~~vere~~
were ~~weer~~

Name _____ Date _____

Rhymes

A rhyme is a word that sounds similar to another. Like *blue / true*. Some words are long and so the rhyme is focused on the end of the word. Like *remember / December*

Pick the best rhyming word for the sentence.

1. Hamilton's a troll. He lives in a ___**hole**___ .
   hole, bowl

2. Rosa the racoon, slept under the ___**moon**___ .
   spoon, moon

3. The color is red, on top of his ___**head**___ .
   bed, head

4. When Hamilton is sad, no body is ___**glad**___ .
   mad, glad

5. How would you know, when the wind will ___**blow**___ .
   blow, grow

6. When the tree is gone, it is bright at ___**dawn**___ .
   yawn, dawn

7. The birds would fly, in the ___**sky**___ .
   try, sky

8. Rudy lost his hat, Merle lost his ___**mat**___ .
   mat, fat

9. They looked at the ground. They looked all ___**around**___ .
   found, around

10. Fiona is sweet. She's quick on her ___**feet**___ .
    beat, feet

Name _____ Date _____

Hamilton Troll
meets
RUDY RAT

Read the sentences below and determine which is right and which is wrong? Write your answer in the blank. A sample has been done for you.

Rudy Rat is being mean to others. ____wrong____

Rosa Racoon tells Hamilton Troll. ____right____

1. Rudy Rat popped Rosa's mushroom ball. ____wrong____

2. Rosa and the children invite Rudy to play. ____right____

3. Rudy Rat teases Diggory Armadillo. ____wrong____

4. Rudy trips little Timmy in the hall. ____wrong____

5. Hamilton asks the children to talk to Rudy. ____right____

Name _____ Date _____

Hamilton Troll
meets
RUDY RAT

Right or Wrong

Read the sentences below and determine which is right and which is wrong? Write your answer in the blank. A sample has been done for you.

1. A group of children push another child. ___wrong___

2. You ask a child who is alone to join you. ___right___

3. A child breaks another child's toys. ___wrong___

4. You ignore a child who is crying. ___wrong___

5. You put your PAWS together for friendship. ___right___

6. You let someone borrow a crayon. ___right___

7. You draw on someone else's drawing without

   asking for permission. ___wrong___

Name _____ Date _____

Hamilton Troll
meets
RUDY RAT

Right or Wrong

Read the sentences below and determine which is right and which is wrong? Write your answer in the blank. A sample has been done for you.

1. You introduce yourself to a new child. _____right_____

2. You see a bully and tell a teacher. _____right_____

3. Someone tells you to do something that you think may be wrong and you do it anyway. _____wrong_____

4. You tell a child they would be cool if they picked on another child. _____wrong_____

5. You tell your parents someone is being mean when they are not being mean. _____right_____

Name: _____ Date: _____

Fill in the beginning consonant letter for each word.
Draw a line from the word to the matching picture.

_T_ roll

_R_ accoon

_M_ ouse

_B_ ee

_S_ quirrel

_D_ inosaur

B D M R S T

CROSSWORD PUZZLE

WORD BANK

DOME
FLOP
HOOT
POLLEN
SPRITE
SQUIRREL
STICKNUT
TROLL

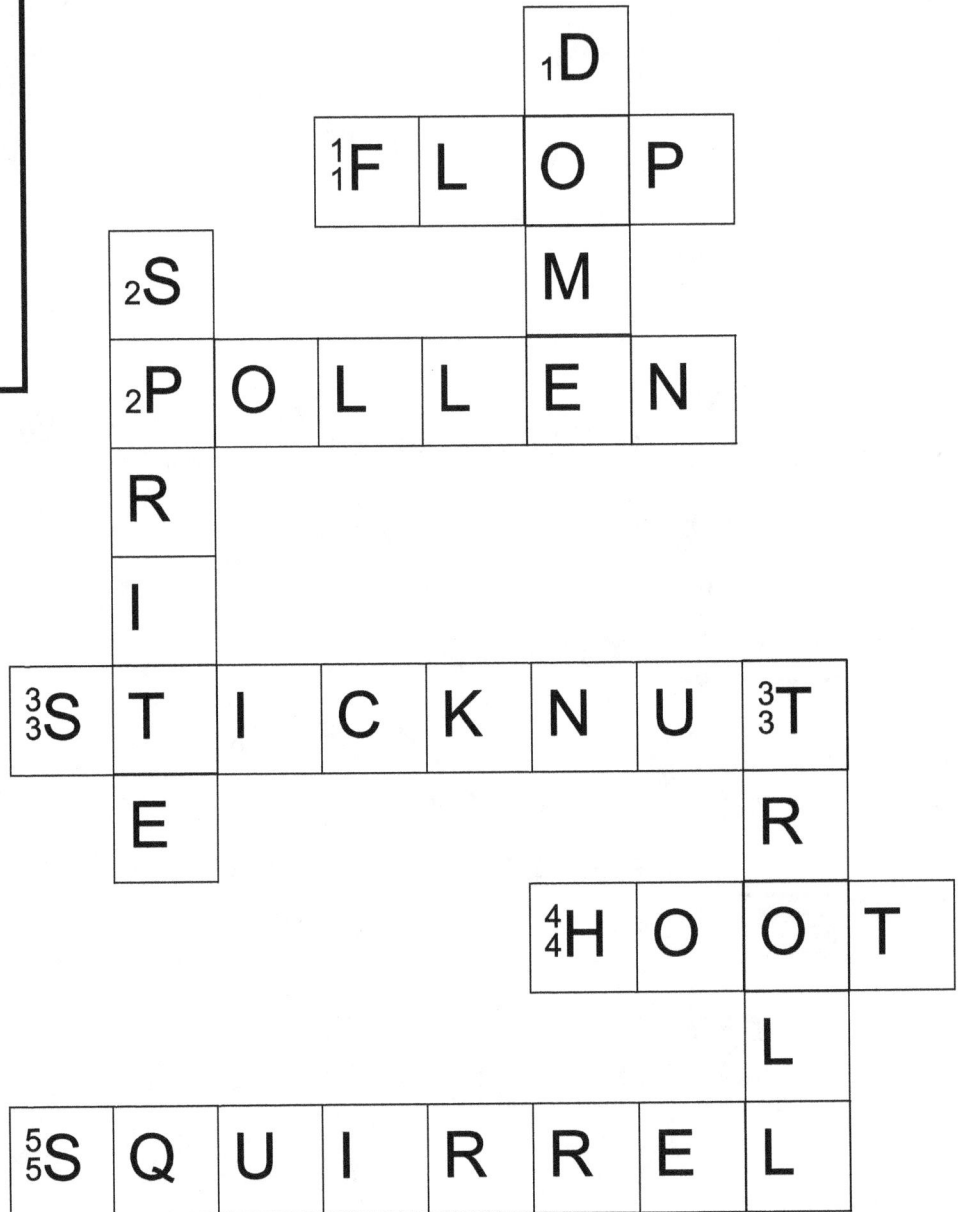

```
              D
         F L O P
       S   M
       P O L L E N
       R
       I
    S T I C K N U T   T
       E             R
              H O O T
                    L
    S Q U I R R E L
```

ACROSS

1. THE SIGN IS CALLED HIDE AWAY ____

2. BARNEY BEE LOVES ____

3. THE GAME THEY PLAY IS ____

4. WHITAKER OWL LEARNS TO ____

5. CHATTERTON IS A ____

DOWN

1. THE LEAVES MAKE
   THE SHAPE OF A ____

2. PINK LIGHT ____

3. HAMILTON IS A ____

MATH WORKSHEET

ANSWERS

Name: _____   Date: _____

Hamilton Troll meets
Barney Bee

Math
Counting Flowers

Barney Bee now needs to keep track of how many flowers he eats per day if he wants to keep flying. Look at the chart to see how many flowers he ate from each day and what color they were. Then answer the questions below.

Day	Blue	Pink	Yellow
Day 1	4	4	3
Day 2	2	5	4
Day 3	0	6	5
Day 4	5	2	8

1. How many flowers did he eat from on day 2?

   2+5+4=11

2. How many blue flowers did he eat total?

   4+2+0+5=11

3. How many pink and blue flowers did he eat on day 3?

   0+6=6

4. Did he eat any blue flowers on day 3?

   No

5. On day 4 Barney Bee fell from the sky. What did he do different from the first three days?

   Day1 = 11
   Day 2 = 11
   Day 3 = 11
   Day 4 = 15
   He at 4 too many flowers.

Name: _____ Date: _____

Hamilton Troll meets

Barney Bee

Math

1. How many stripes are on Barney Bee's tail?

   7

2. How many stripes are white?

   3

3. How many arms does Barney Bee have?

   6

4. If there are 5 flowers and Barney eats nectar out of two, how many flowers does he have left?

   5 - 2 = 3

5. To keep Barney flying, he needs to do 5 jumping jacks for every flower he eats from. How many flowers can he eat from if he does 25 jumping jacks?

   25 / 5 = 5

Hamilton Troll meets Skeeter Skunk

Counting Frogs

Hamilton Troll and friends counted the cheering frogs at the Stick-Nut game for the last four days. Look at the chart to see how many frogs they saw each day. Then answer the questions.

Cheering Frogs

Day	Frogs
Day 1	5
Day 2	8
Day 3	10
Day 4	7

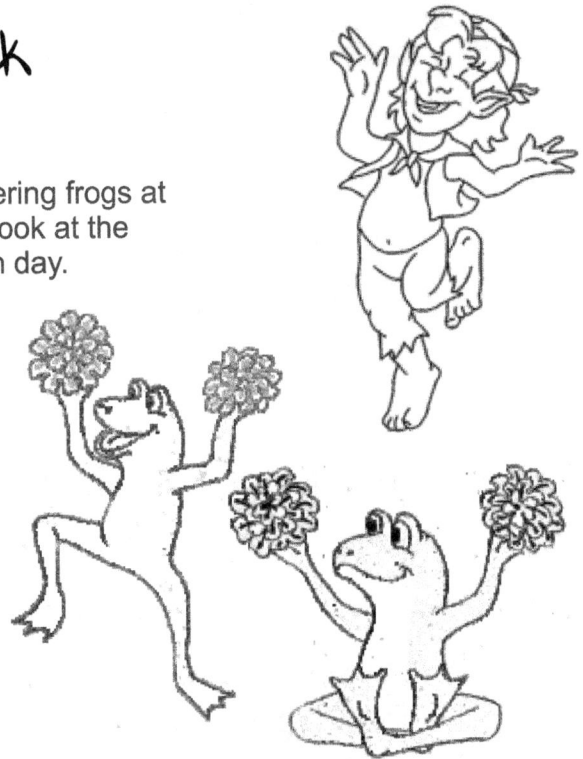

How many frogs did Hamilton and friends see in all?

___30___ frogs in all

How many fewer frogs did they see on day 1 versus day 4?

___2___ fewer frogs

How many more frogs did Hamilton and friends see in day 3 versus day 1?

___5___ more frogs

Name _____ Date _____

Math
Addition

1) How many fingers are visible on Hamilton's waving hand? _____ 4 _____

2) How many fingers are on one of your hands? _____ 5 _____

3) Add your answers, how many fingers
are on Hamilton's hand and your hand. _____ $4 + 5 = 9$

4) How many ears are on the bunnies above? _____ 4 _____

5) How many tails are on the animals above? _____ 8 _____

4) Add your answers, how many bunny
ears and animal tails are there? _____ $8 + 4 = 12$

Name _____ Date _____

Math
Addition

1) How many squirrels are there above? ___4___

2) How many birds are there total? ___6___

3) Add the total of squirrels
   and birds together. ___4 + 6 = 10___

4) How many bugs are there? ___5___

5) Add how many bugs and
   squirrels there are total? ___5 + 4 = 9___

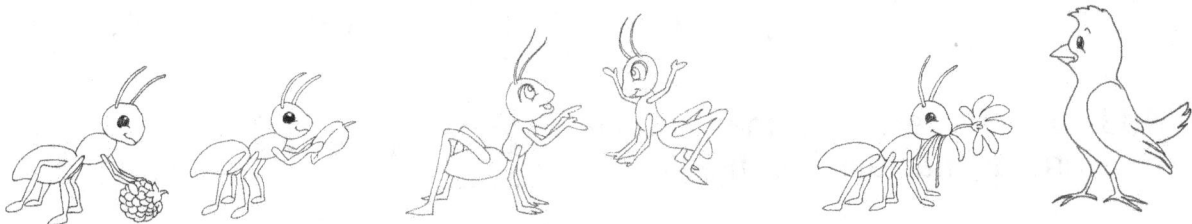

Name: _____   Date: _____

Hamilton Troll meets
ELWOOD WOODPECKER

1. How many stars does Elwood Woodpecker see?

    10

2. How many flower petals are there total?

    $8 \times 4 = 32$

3. Looking at the pictures below, How many worms does Elwood Woodpecker get to eat?

    8

4. How many fish are swimming around the beaver brothers?

    8

Name: _____ Date: _____

Hamilton Troll meets
ELWOOD WOODPECKER

Math
Subtraction

1. If Elwood Woodpecker eats three worms. How many are left?

$$7 - 3 = 4$$

2. If Hamilton Troll picks 9 flowers and gives 3 to Elwood and 2 to Baxter Beaver, how many will he have left?

4

$$9 - 3 = 6$$
$$6 - 2 = 4$$

3. If Baxter and Boswell each cut down two trees, how many will be left standing in the scene below?

5

$$9 - 2 = 7$$
$$7 - 2 = 5$$

Name: _____ Date: _____

Hamilton Troll meets
ELWOOD WOODPECKER

1. If Boswell Beaver uses 2 trees to make a dam, how many dams can he make if he has 10 trees?

_____2_____ x _____10_____ = _____20_____

2. If Elwood Woodpecker eats seven bugs a day, how many will he eat in a week?

_____7_____ x _____7_____ = _____49_____

3. If Hamilton Troll teaches three animals about petrified wood and they each teach three animals, how many animals will know about petrified wood?

_____3_____ x _____3_____ = _____9_____

Name: _____ Date: _____

Hamilton Troll meets
ELWOOD WOODPECKER

1. Baxter and Boswell Beaver each cut down three logs. How many logs do they have total?

$$\underline{\quad 3 \quad} \; \text{x} \; \underline{\quad 2 \quad} = \underline{\quad 6 \quad}$$

2. Elwood Woodpecker has three butterflies land on his head. How many heads are there?

$$\begin{array}{r} 3 \\ \hline \text{x} \quad 1 \\ \hline = \quad 3 \end{array}$$

3. How many flower petals are there in all? Fill in the blanks with the question and answer.

$$\underline{\quad 4 \quad} \; \text{x} \; \underline{\quad 3 \quad} = \underline{\quad 12 \quad}$$

Name: _____ Date: _____

Hamilton Troll meets
ELWOOD WOODPECKER

Beavers build dams in rivers and streams. These dams are their home. The dams also create homes for fish, frogs, turtles and other aquatic life.

Why do you think aquatic life likes to live around beaver dams?

River is not moving.   It is quiet.
Plants can grow there.   It is safe.

What are three things you need to make a beaver dam?

___ Trees ___ + ___ River ___ + ___ Beavers ___ = **Beaver Dam**

Draw a beaver dam below.

Hamilton Troll Curriculum
www.HamiltonTroll.com

FUN STUFF

ANSWERS

Hamilton Troll loves watching the ants work.

He wishes he could see the tunnels within an ant pile and go inside and explore. But what if he got lost? Help this ant get through the maze by going under and over in the tunnels to get to the other side.

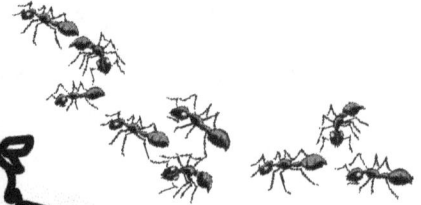

Start

End

Did you know that trees have rings?

Not like gold rings, but lines that look like circles. These circles are called rings, like you see below, and if you count the rings, you will know how many years that tree had been alive.

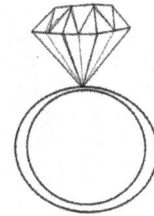

Make your way through this tree stumps rings to get to the center.

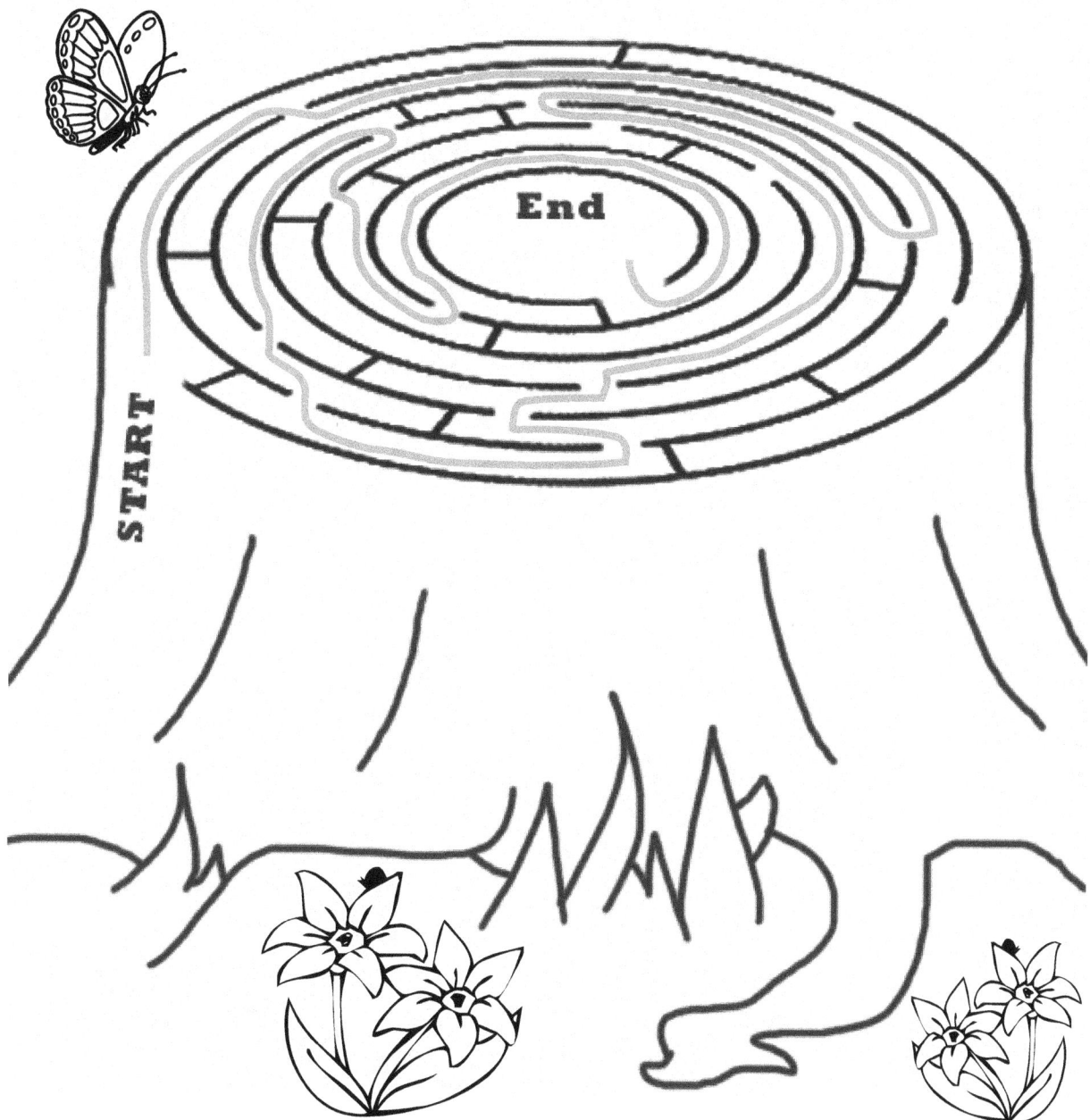

START

End

When the Wind Blows...

it makes it difficult for birds to fly. They get caught in wind currents which spiral them around. Help this bird make it through the wind currents to get to the other side.

Finish

Start

Trolls are usually hard to find.
But in this word search they are very easy.
How many times can you find the
word TROLL in this search?

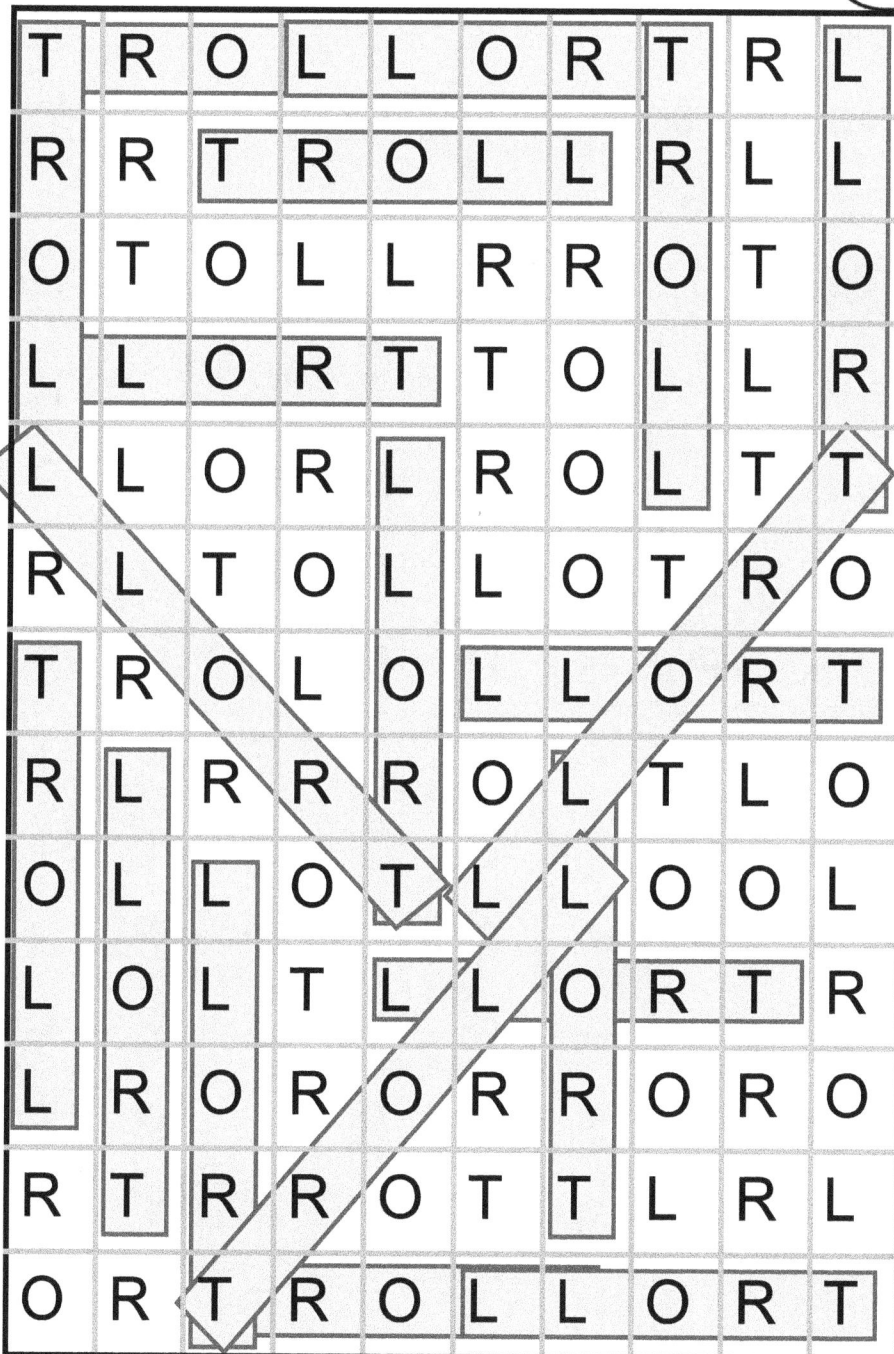

T	R	O	L	L	O	R	T	R	L
R	R	T	R	O	L	L	R	L	L
O	T	O	L	L	R	R	O	T	O
L	L	O	R	T	T	O	L	L	R
L	L	O	R	L	R	O	L	T	T
R	L	T	O	L	L	O	T	R	O
T	R	O	L	O	L	L	O	R	T
R	L	R	R	R	O	L	T	L	O
O	L	L	O	T	L	L	O	O	L
L	O	L	T	L	L	O	R	T	R
L	R	O	R	O	R	R	O	R	O
R	T	R	R	O	T	T	L	R	L
O	R	T	R	O	L	L	O	R	T

How many
times did
you find
the word
TROLL?

_____19_____

Pink Light Sprite

Will always be around but will be out of sight... which makes her hard to find. But in this word search you can find the word SPRITE a whole lot of times!

Haw many times can you find SPRITE? | 15

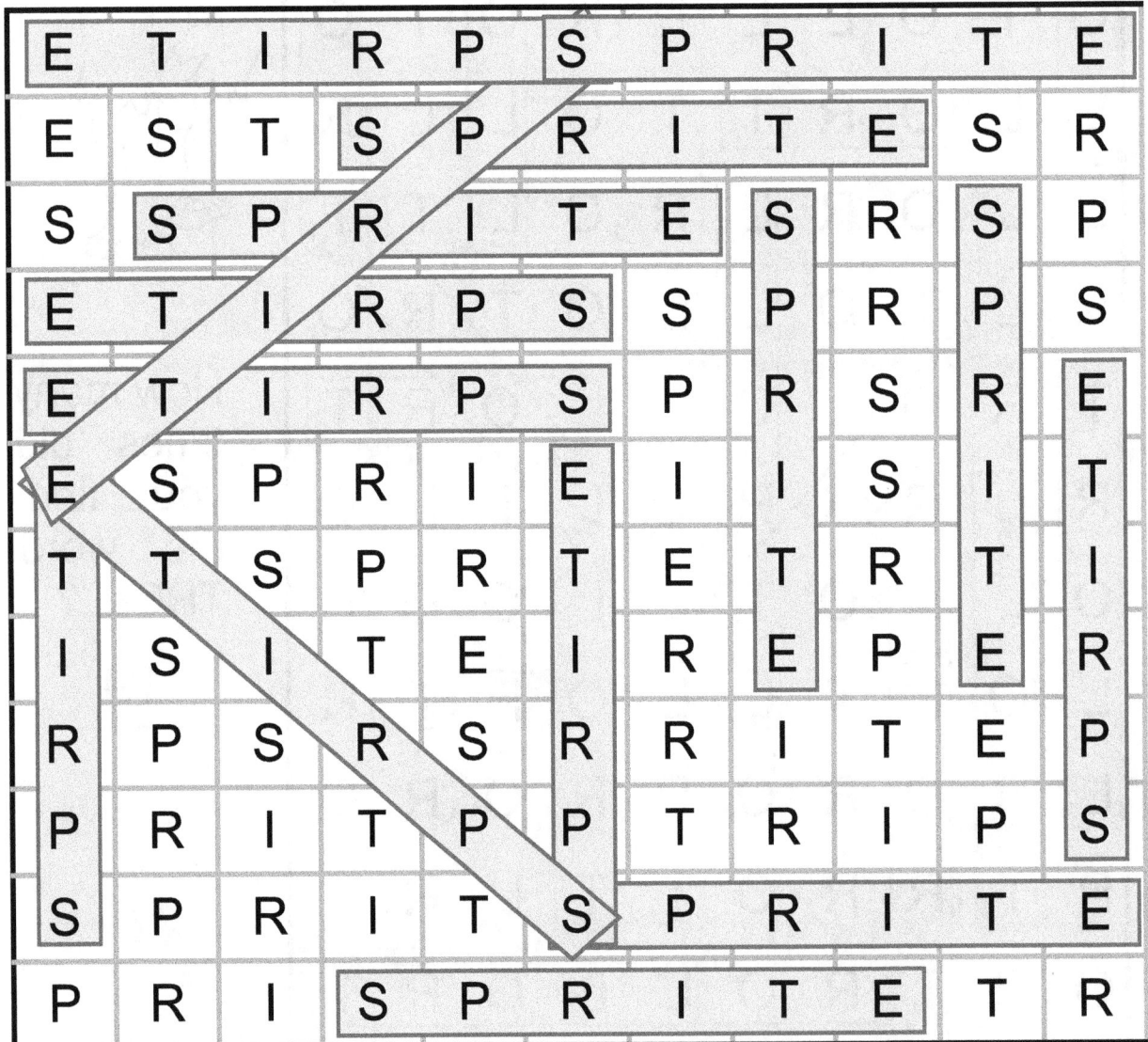

Grid 1

S	Q	U	I	R	R	E	L	K	T
K	K	O	W	L	A	E	E	C	H
E	N	U	T	R	L	L	S	I	G
E	L	C	N	U	T	O	P	T	I
T	R	O	L	K	T	I	R	S	L
E	L	W	O	O	D	P	I	T	K
R	C	H	A	M	I	L	T	O	N
B	A	R	N	E	Y	B	E	E	I
R	E	K	A	T	I	H	W	O	P
C	H	A	T	T	E	R	T	O	N

Grid 2

N	A	N	O	T	R	E	C	H	A	T	N
C	A	T	O	O	N	C	H	A	R	O	O
T	H	R	E	N	C	A	R	T	T	N	T
R	H	E	T	R	T	O	O	R	O	C	R
E	R	T	R	E	H	O	E	A	N	H	E
T	H	T	E	T	R	T	N	H	T	A	T
A	T	T	A	T	T	I	H	C	E	T	A
H	A	A	R	A	T	R	O	N	R	T	A
C	R	H	H	C	H	A	T	T	R	O	H
T	A	C	H	A	T	E	R	T	O	N	C

Grid 3

L	I	T	O	N	O	T	L	I	M	A	H
H	A	H	A	M	I	L	T	O	O	N	
N	A	N	H	A	M	I	N	L	O	T	A
O	M	M	A	H	A	M	I	L	T	O	N
T	I	L	I	H	T	H	A	M	L	T	N
L	L	O	T	L	I	M	A	H	I	T	H
I	I	N	I	N	T	H	A	M	M	N	A
M	M	M	A	H	N	O	T	I	A	O	M
A	A	M	I	L	T	O	N	L	H	T	I
H	H	O	N	O	T	L	I	M	A	H	L

Add to your child's education – let them grow up with Hamilton Troll.

Hamilton Troll is an ambassador of education. He is curious, inquisitive, adventurous and most of all fun! He asks questions children tend to ask and they learn through him in these entertaining, award-winning, rhyming stories by Texas author Kathleen J. Shields and illustrators Leigh A. Klug and Carol W. Bryant.

Teachers, Home-schoolers, Mom & Dad; this is an educational story series you will not want to miss out on! Children will be enthralled by the illustrations.

If you read the rhyming stories to them, they will fall in love with them.
If you help teach them the vocabulary words their knowledge will increase.
If you work with them through the activities and curriculum you will make learning fun.

Spend time with Hamilton Troll and when you are ready for a break, check out the interactive website that has games, videos (Troll TV) Did You Know Facts, more information about each character and so much more! There's even shopping for gifts, t-shirts and toys.

There is so much to do in the world of Hamilton Troll - come check it out!

www.HamiltonTroll.com